Confessions of a Pipeman

Also by Gary B. Schrier ...

The History of the Calabash Pipe
The Loewé Pipe Packet

CONFESSIONS
OF A PIPEMAN

An irreverent guide for
today's pipe-smoking man

— SECOND EDITION —

GARY B. SCHRIER

FOREWORD BY MARTY PULVERS

Briar Books Press

Published by Briar Books Press

Photo credits (1): © *Reproduced under license of ...*
   H M Bateman Designs Limited: 53; Condé Nast Publications (Drawing by
   Leonard Dove): 55; William Hamilton/ The New Yorker Collection: 87;
   Mary Evans Picture Library: 49; Garrett Price/ The New Yorker
   Collection: 96; Punch Ltd: 6, 9, 15, 33, 40, 74
Photo credits (2): © *Reproduced courtesy of ...*
   Amazon: 28; Davidoff: 10; Matt Guss: 84; Pakeman, Catto & Carter: 90;
   Neill Archer Roan: 25; Jacek Schmidt: 22; Mr. & Mrs. Albert Schrier: vii;
   Gary B. Schrier: cover, 22, 68, 69, 76, 83, 89, 95, 102, 128

Second Edition

Printed in China

Additional copies of this title and other pipe books may be acquired directly
through the publisher at www.briarbooks.com.

WITH AFFECTION

To my wife, Priscilla, for her
love and for letting me alone
to do my thing

To my sons: Captain Christopher S. Motter, U.S. Army
for engaging the enemy, for making a difference,
a better man; and Master Ben, a warrior in the making

&

Ben Rapaport, for his many contributions

Laurentian Mountains ca. 1933

To my father, Albert Schrier (1923-   )
   A better dad would be unimaginable.

There is nothing to writing. All you do is sit down at a typewriter and bleed.

—Ernest Hemingway

CONTENTS

Foreword

GARY B. SCHRIER is our kind of pipeman, or at least my kind of pipeman. The "pipe" part of the word is covered by his devotion to our favorite hobby, pipes, pipe tobacco and pipe smoking. A good number of people qualify on the basis of these criteria. It's the "man" part of the word where Gary shines, and what makes this book glisten. Gary is knowledgeable, experienced and forthright ("honest" would do just as well) to the point of being politically incorrect. Good for him and good for us. He is not afraid to tell his version of the truth, and that is becoming a very rare commodity, as we are all being buried by verbal bullshit (and in this instance, I cannot think of another word that would be more apt).

For the aspiring pipe smoker, there is no source that can educate and inform as this book. It would not be going an inch too far to call this a *critical* resource for that incipient pipe smoker, because the information contained herein is not going to be readily available anywhere else, and without it, the beginner just might well lose his/her way and give up on the wonderful world of pipe smoking. In fact, that is the major problem with this book … it might not be put into the hands of the novice in time to save him. And aside from us, and the support we can get from a book such as *Confessions*, there's not much motivation for somebody to put in the effort necessary to become a pipeman. I suppose, then, it falls to us to make certain that a book like this—a true guide—gets to those who need it most: your young friend who wants to take up pipe smoking and simply doesn't know how to begin. For most would-be pipe smokers, walking into a decent tobacco shop is too daunting a task, and so the alternative to buying a drugstore pipe and some gawd-awful-tasting tobacco is the default, leading to a very disappointing, pipe-ending experience. With the contents of Gary's book digested, a beginner can confidently walk into the most specialized store in the world and not feel overwhelmed and scared. I wish I had had this book when I was 18 years old. It was only by luck that I overcame that first terrible pipe shop experience and managed to prevail. Luck and, bless the pipe gods, latakia.

Confessions might be the perfect title for this book. Earlier, I called it a guide, and it is that, but written in such a frank manner that one could imagine lesser men than the author limiting his strongly expressed insights (they are opinions, yes, but opinions born of experience and deserving more consideration than faith-based opinions) uttered to a close friend or confessor. Fortunately for us, Gary is willing to make a clean breast of it and suffer whatever criticism might arise. If we're open to him, we derive the benefit of his courage.

This is not to say that I agree with all he offers and, clearly, he does not expect us to agree with him 100 percent. What he probably does expect, and has the right to expect, is that we have a sound reason for disagreeing. To disagree simply because something he says isn't warm or friendly sounding is not a good reason. Unsubstantiated criticism carries no weight in the marketplace of thought and debate.

In that very same vein, Gary is no cockeyed optimist. He knows that pipe smokers are dinosaurs. He has no illusions. You will not be coddled. You will not be told pipe smoking is easy, that you can learn to do it well in a short period of time, say, three years. No. He tells you that you might get the hang of it in five years or so. Well, I'm sorry … he's right, although I'd say that in this instance he's very optimistic, but then, I have always been considered a little, shall we say, "slower" than the average person.

I must make one objection to Gary's observations, when he says that cigars equate with success as opposed to pipes, which projects the image of sagacity and kindness. Gary and I do not agree on what constitutes success. I think that no amount of money and its trappings could make me feel successful. But, if people I love and admire think of me as both kind and sagacious, I would feel very successful, indeed, as successful as any man could possibly be. I don't believe in letting others define success for me. I'll bet I can persuade Gary to agree.

In talking about the positive impact this book could have on someone contemplating the pipe, it shouldn't be imagined that there is nothing here for the experienced smoker. There is everything for that class of citizen as well: the rules of courtesy, the value (or absence of value) of cellaring tobacco, the way to pack your smoking kit for trips, the mania surrounding the health effects of smoking, pipe myths etc.; all this is covered as nowhere else with confidence and confirmation. How to describe the vast range of critical material that Gary covers? I probably can't, but if I tell you that this book is the pipe amalgam of Miss Manners, Dear Abby, and the American version of Georges Herment (see Gary's required reading list in chapter 4), I wouldn't be far off, although *Confessions* is, of course, more than the sum of those three parts. Its style is unique, and more, its substance is sage.

If this book is read by the right people, it'll do its job. Its direct honesty will get the potential pipeman past all, or almost all, the roadblocks that, for a new adherent, eventually kill the urge to smoke a pipe. It will position the novice to enjoy a life of pipe smoking. When read by the accomplished, it will make a more congenial, thoughtful, wiser and happier colleague. That promise of keeping our hobby alive and emotionally healthy makes this book a worthwhile investment: buy it, read and read it again, and also gift it to those we'd like to bring along on our wonderful pipe-smoking ride. *Confessions* is in your hands. Read it and enjoy!

—Marty Pulvers

Preface to the Second Edition

WITH the release of *Confessions* Christmas Eve 2008, I was once again entering the realm of publishing, as I had done two-and-one-half years earlier with the release of my first book, *The History of the Calabash Pipe*. The two books, of course, are wholly different. Frankly, I was expecting much more from *Confessions* than I ever did with the calabash book.

The idea for a second book was easy to fathom—I needed it. My work on the *Calabash* left me with a routine which I could not easily abandon: the research, the writing, the editing, the producing, and so on. The concept for the work, on the other hand, was less easy to come by. But, eventually, I gave a difficult birth to the idea of a confessional. I saw a great need for a better understanding of the pipe smoker, who he is, but equally as important, who he could and should become. Men who smoke tobacco in pipes, and many more who quietly try but fail—were in need of a guide, not one based on some silly pedantic treatment of how to load a pipe, light a pipe, smoke a pipe, and finally, to clean a pipe—how tedious—but one of a much broader and realistic encompassment. It was to become a lifestyle guide, because for most who take pleasure in the pipe, it *is* so much more of a lifestyle than a hobby.

Some two years since its release, I am still chided by some who are close enough to me to say their words to my face and yet several more who must do it long-distance fashion. Those who tendered the harshest reviews have since been forgotten, their names stricken forever from the mailing list. To those who have extended helpful comments, I am most grateful to you. The best of the best reviews, which I did hear on more than a few occasions, was that the book ended too quickly. To all of you who wanted more, this book is for you, the new material amounting to fifty percent more text, illustrations, and photographs. The expectation from the marketing department at Briar Books press is that both editions are now considered a set, that those holding the first must now acquire the second, that anything less is unfathomable and silly.

At the outset, I never held out hope for a second edition. There were a few niggling corrections forthcoming, and those could be attended to properly with subsequent printings. But I never thought for a moment there was any material I had omitted with the first edition. I was wrong—six chapters worth. And so, I began with chapter 7, with a defense of and homage to Dunhill and what made them survive when few others did in their original form. I laid down further barrage to aromatic tobacco in chapter 15, Cavendish. With chapter 19, Heart of Hearts, I do more justice to the realm of anti-smoking legislation and what the pipeman can do to protect himself. In chapter 21, I turn my focus to the thoughts of others, their quotes—some better known than others—and their implications on various aspects of the pipe-smoking lifestyle. Then, with the following chapter, I do a mildly comedic performance with "You Might be a Pipeman if ...." And finally, with chapter 23, there's the sobering look at the eventuality of death and the task of dispersing of one's collection prior to.

There was one very large change to the trade in the between-edition years. The realization that Dunhill-branded mixtures would no longer be made available in North America came as a heavy blow to American pipemen. That I had based my "right tobacco" or English benchmark on Dunhill's My Mixture 965, in particular, became a rather looming structural issue that needed tending to if the second edition was to continue being of good use, chiefly to the newer pipe-smoking man.

The balance of the book remains largely unchanged, though through the economies of overseas printing, I was able to print many of the images—the many drole illustrations—in their original color. Perhaps less noticeable, was a change in the text stock and finish to the cover.

There are those who believe *Confessions* is a pretentious and demanding little book replete with edicts and acceptable styles; and that such a primer is unnecessary. They say that Schrier thinks pipe smoking is altogether dead. They are not altogether incorrect making such observations. But those with such views come from the dullards and naïve among the coterie, who see no further into what I wrote than their own simplistic agenda, that of a hobby filled with happiness and sunshine and room for nothing else. That this author cares deeply for the lifestyle of the pipeman, however emblematic of the dying breed, should never been in question.

—GBS
Burley, Washington

Preface

THERE aren't many pipe smokers around anymore. The demise of the pipe—the briar pipe, the one everyone's uncle or grandfather was known to have smoked—has been hovering over North American society like a dooming rain cloud for the last several decades. Since the 1950s perhaps? The '60s? I don't know and don't believe an esoteric bit of research such as this has ever been sanctioned by a university or the tobacco industry to figure it all out, because no one really cares about the pipe smoker. So you should ask: why this book? Why write about pipes if they're no longer a part of popular culture (if our uncles and grandfathers could ever be viewed in such light) and, more importantly, that there's too little a market left to sell to?

I wrote my first book on pipes and self-published it in the spring of 2006. It met with critical acclaim, and there was a run (not at all like a run on a bank which ain't so good)—all 250 copies—but I had to nearly sell my soul to have it printed. The *History of the Calabash Pipe* was a big deal just like that pipe used to be 90 years ago. The calabash isn't so big anymore. Neither is the briar pipe, but less so. The fact that smoking is associated with cancer may have something to do with it, but I think only a small part.

For what remains of these tobacco pipe-smoking men in the civilized world I write this book. This group of pipe-men, as I like to call them, are split into two distinct camps: those who smoke briar and those who are briar-smoking hobbyists. I believe my book will appeal to both groups. Unlike my last work, which was neatly splashed with photographs depicting nuance upon nuance, this book has none save the cameo appearance of the author or drole cartoons scattered to and fro. I've been told that the pipe collector needs visuals. If this is true, this book may be tough to get through. Do your best.

Oh, I've made certain you'll get your purchase price out of the deal, but you must know that I've been well schooled in book writing for pipe smokers and collectors, and understand this: there is no money in the deal. So believe that this writer of print-on-demand press is, sadly, no whore for a publisher's cash advance, but another hard-trying writer—a pipe-smoking one by God!—with a story to tell to an uncertain audience. I hope you find I tell it well.

—GBS

Introduction

Confess— *v.* **1.** To disclose or acknowledge (something damaging or inconvenient to oneself). **2.** To concede the truth or validity of; admit. **3.** To acknowledge belief or faith in. **4.** To make known (one's sin), especially to a priest for absolution.

The American Heritage Dictionary

ANYONE can smoke a cigarette. From an early age you see friends and strangers smoking them. When it's your turn to see what you should naturally be doing as well, it's understandable to assume the innateness of the process and, for the most part, you'd be right. Lighting them; holding them; puffing them; it all seems like a natural extension of the human form. Those first hauls are usually miserable, but in short order you've mastered the art. Certainly much easier than learning to tie your shoes. But the knack of puffing away on a fag needs little, if any, formal training, other than just coming of age and hanging out with your school-mates. Not so with the pipe. Why is that?

Pipes are for old men. At least that's the youthful perspective. And when you're supposed to be experimenting in grade school, the last thing you wanted to be seen as was a grown-up. Pipes have never been cool; sophisticated looking, yes, but that image just doesn't register until much later in life. Coupled with the reality that in the mainstream of civilization pipes are nowhere to be seen; the practice of smoking tobacco in a pipe is anachronistic. So, the scene today is that there are young men of all ages at a crossroads in their life when they feel compelled to act out, to abandon the cigarette or, perhaps, have come to the realization that a pipe should be considered. They have reached that age when their confidence will support them through the trials, but have either vague recollections of seeing someone smoke a pipe or no experience whatsoever and, thus, the *how to* of getting on with it remains a mystery. As Mark Twain was to have said some 125 years ago, "everybody wants to smoke a pipe but nobody knows how to go about it."

Invariably, most who sally forth fail miserably. The experience with the pipe is short-lived, and a partly consumed pouch of tobacco tucked away in a seldom-used desk drawer is a sign of a trial never to be repeated. Undeniably, this has for so long been one of the greatest contributing factors as to why the pipe was never hugely popular for any extended length of time, unlike its vastly more popular cousins, the cigarette and cigar.

Ultimately, as most everything else is in life, learning the practice of smoking a pipe is entirely up to you. If you purchased this book for such purpose you will feel cheated because this is not one of those *Dummy* or *Idiot* guides that proliferate the self-help section of your town's few remaining bookstores. Despair not, because there are quaint little picture books, most now long out-of-print, that do just that. This book, on the other hand, will tell you everything else you need to know.

Look, if you think the pipe is singularly about smoking tobacco, you're wrong; there's so much more. What you're holding is a guide, a never-before-written manual for the novice about to join the rarefied breed of pipeman*, and for the consummate pipe smoker and pipe collector who never quite got it right, because of his stubbornness or lack of knowledge.

Through these pages you will learn that a pipe is not just a pipe; through its presence and proper use your actions will take on new meaning and you will derive a sense of satisfaction on an order you could not have heretofore imagined. Consider yourself fortunate. For the simple price of admission you have in your hands a collection of confessions from this hardened pipeman based on experiences not so easily attained.

With this slight book, as disciplined as you find its directives, and as immodest and opinionated as you will surely find its author, you will not find cause to dither in agreeing with or immediately acting out on the advice dished out at the appropriate moment. If you are determined to succeed at the pipe, you will: this book promises you that! (If you're not completely satisfied, you are, my good fellow, not pipe-worthy. Pass the book on to a cherished friend who himself needs such enlightenment as this book proffers.)

---

* This is the first use in this book of the term *pipeman* and, I believe, in any other smoking-related title for that matter, a term that simplistically refers to a man who smokes a pipe. Its meaning should be self-evident within the context of this prose, but it's formally defined in chapter 2. Clearly, the word is sexist. With less regard for the appearance of political correctness and more thoughtfulness toward opportunity of the sexes as to who actually smokes a pipe, I gave careful consideration to the use of alternate words including, pipe-woman, pipe-person, pipester, pipe smoker, and even piper. I was uncomfortable with most except for pipe smoker, an established term that is gender-neutral, so its use is sprinkled throughout the book. Liberal-minded readers, I would hope, including women, especially those who smoke pipes, will not take offense at my greater use of the more effectual term, pipeman. You see, men smoke pipes; men have forever been associated with the pipe; and the word is masculine, evoking all sorts of emotions. Women also smoke pipes, and have for centuries, but their numbers have always been miniscule by comparison, particularly in North America. If you consider yourself to be a *pipewoman*, more power to you. Everything in this book could be applied equally to women, and I hope that it will. So while this book is written for anyone with an interest in the topic, know that it is defined by the majority behind its history and use to present day, the pipeman.

Here, look at this. You'll learn a little of the history of what the classic pipeman used to be like and what led to his demise. If you're an apprentice in the art of pipe smoking, you'll learn that smoke shops aren't what they used to be, and the last place you should look to get started. You'll be given a reading list of essential tomes that will carry your education beyond the intent of this book and broaden your outlook not only on smoking, but also for reading's sake as a long-forgotten pastime since Internet porn and YouTube took over everyone's discretionary time. And, reluctantly, I am dragged into a review of your manners, such that a whole new set of demands are now upon you as a smoker. Chapter 5 on etiquette and chapter 6 on savoir-faire will not only keep you on the straight course and out of harm's way, but will also instruct you in the ability to say and do anything with a level of confidence and panache you did not realize you were capable of.

And more. You'll see that all pipes are not created equal; some pipes are better for certain environs; some pipes should only be for purposes of admiring; and some should never be looked at twice. You'll discover— perhaps with some incredulity—that there is only one style of mixture to smoke and only one pipe style in which to smoke it. And, since we humans move about, there is a brief treatise on traveling with your pipe stuff.

Finally, there are chapters on collecting, pipe clubs, smoking rooms, smoker's health, comedy, and, eventually, even death—not of the pipe but of the man. Collecting, you will learn, is sheer folly for many who undertake the distraction, but it does have its admirers who have found the trick to keeping it real and smart. With pipe clubs, you'll wonder why they're such well-kept secrets and an indispensable gathering place for pipemen of all ages, professions, and trades. A smoking room? Well, the pipeman simply cannot exist in any modicum of comfort, safety, or style without one. With smoker's health, believe it or not, there's good news: life not death! I follow this with my views on the many established facts of Smokedom so sanctified by pipemen. Realizing at this time that some levity was required, and knowing full well that I am unable to effectively deliver the simplest of jokes, I spun a good-natured comedic look at all of us pipemen, who we think we are, and what others' perceptions are of us. Lastly, as death is at the bottom of every bowl of tobacco, so too is the eventuality of the pipeman's demise and the matter of a careful review of estate planning.

Through this book and your own attempts at mastery of the briar pipe, you will learn that—not unlike joining the navy—the pipe will take you places that will enrich your passage through life and the people you touch along the way. *Bon voyage et bonne chance!*

1

Pipe Smoking Today

The fear of death follows from the fear of life. A man who lives fully is prepared to die at any time.

—Mark Twain

BE forewarned: pipe smoking is dead. And the bulk of pipes are buried deep in the rubbish heaps of civilization or tucked neatly away from public scrutiny in museums, carefully catalogued as relics of another time, clearly never to see the light of day, let alone a renaissance. It's true. I should know, because I am one of the last pipemen. I am 49 years old and of the last generation that will have known of the pipe and its practice. I do not lament the passing of the pipe, for I'm selfish. I have used it well for much of the first part of my life and will continue to reap its benefits for as long as I choose.

Dinosaurs and an array of other frightening creatures once roamed this planet. That they are no longer among our race is, in general, I believe, a good thing. They had their time, but their time came and went. So, too, did buffalo that once roamed the prairies in carpets of moving dust and the Indians on painted ponies who lived among them. All gone. And ball-bearing manufacturing plants in the United States; and affordable shoes built with steel shanks and leather soles; and receptionists in office lobbies; and Blue Diamond Smokehouse-brand almonds served in tiny packets aboard airliners; and metal tubes that held toothpaste that would often rupture. Things, all of them, some more noble and romantic than others, but all still objects permanently retired, or in such disuse as to have been forgotten. As is the pipe.

What strangeness to gaze upon a pipe smoker in the streets, n'est-ce pas? The well-stocked and, especially important, well-informed tobacconist— another relic from a not-too-distant time—is always a surprise when encountered in one's travels. Hollywood reminds us that there was something different before. In those old movies the stars smoked pipes, and they probably did so because they were smokers off set as well. Our politicians smoked pipes. And many pretty faces were smoking in the pages of magazine advertisements. The working man smoked! The medical doctor smoked! He smoked his pipe at work and at home. No one paid mind. It's as if he were wearing a hat or carrying a particularly distinguished Malacca-handled umbrella. And there once was the businessman who offered an associate or client visiting his office a cigar from a humidor on the desk, or Scotch from a drawer or cabinet laid with a set of crystal decanters.

But cigarettes are everywhere. Repulsive little sticks, loved by their disciples, yet at the same time, so much reviled by a health-conscious citizenry and government alike. The blessed little pipe has neither to show it the independent attention it deserves. Shame on the cigarette smoker! If I had a nickel for every cigarette butt or bit of cellophane wrapping that litters, I'd buy the cigarette factories and convert them to pipe-tobacco factories. But I digress into the dark side of smoking and my peevishness on the cancerous matter. Suffice to say pipes were around before cigarettes, but for perhaps the last 80 or 90 years, a person would almost invariably select a cigarette over a pipe without due consideration. A shame, really, because the pipe is in a class by itself. The pipe lost the product war because it was poorly designed and poorly marketed. The cigarette was cheaper, more convenient, delivered a mild drug, nicotine—actually a poisonous alkaloid—and, so important to the arrested development of the pipe, it became socially acceptable and enjoyed by women. Had the cigarette never emerged to flood society with its ruinous benefits one can only imagine where pipe smoking would stand today.

It wasn't enough for the cigarette to eclipse the pipe, but, of late, it now is inextricably associated through legislation across almost all civilized countries. The anti-smoking movement has swept the world and, I firmly believe, it is here for the duration. Because cigar and pipe smokers knew that their numbers were small, they were destined to be sucked into the vacuum of propaganda that all tobacco and smoking were bad for your health. In point of fact, tobacco is ruinous to one's health, but not when used in moderation. If not already, soon it will be fact that the average American child or adult is clinically obese and at great risk of contracting diabetes. So what should society do with Doritos, McDonald's restaurants, or the miles of aisles of supermarket shelves with fat-laden, sugar-saturated food? And heavens, let's not bounce the discussion to the woeful effects of alcohol abuse.

The pipeman knows all too well the laws and ordinances by which he must now abide. Gone forever are the pleasurable moments of sipping a drink in a pub accompanied by your loyal pipe. Almost stricken from memory are the days when smoking in the office was permitted; when a public building was meant to denote an edifice for purposes of government and not now to include all privately held commercial establishments—even private clubs! The lines have been purposefully distorted to achieve the goals of the nanny state.

Through it all, somehow, pipe smoking survives. Looking for the pipeman, you'll occasionally catch a glimpse of him. He'll be in his car, an elderly gent and wearing a Trilby hat. Outside town he might be behind the wheel of an F-150, a tradesman. A city park is a unique place to see a great cross-section of society, and though your chances are slight, it would not be out of place to see a rugged-looking average Joe; pipe firmly clenched in his mouth; smoke emanating in sizable bursts; faithful pooch tugging alongside.

The tobacconist. Against increasing odds a few decent ones hang on. (What I define as decent will be investigated in chapter 3.) They're there, usually in and around larger cities in states that have punitive smoking laws and those without. There, the pipeman will sit, protected from the din of the street, and enjoy a bowl. Chances are he's a regular and knows what's what.

You'll be exceedingly fortunate to reside within easy reach of the classic 90's cigar bar. A finer place to smoke indoors as this is unlikely. Though the pipeman would be the strange creature among such aficionados of the Churchill, Hemingway and Lonsdale—even those who claim they can spot a fake Cuban (90 percent of them smuggled into the States are!)—they are usually gracious and accommodating toward the pipeman. Perchance they pity him and take him in from the cold.

If you vacation in the forests by backpack, or paddle the rivers and lakes by canoe, lucky be you to cross paths with the 'ol timer. He's the woodsman who will know the pipe well. He may be a hard-bitten local or a worldly explorer, and he knows things from other lands and cultures.

Closer in, and now well past his prime, possibly spry, probably rather sedentary, you may still be blessed with a father, uncle or grandfather who has lived in different times and places where he took the pipe. Maybe he still does.

These pipemen, here and in different places, though their numbers be inconsequential to the demographer, the satisfaction of smoking tobacco in a pipe is, still, to them, a lifestyle. Beyond the obvious and his position in life, what defines this pipeman? Who is he, really, and is he of a special breed?

If you read much of what has been written on pipes and the men who smoke them, you'll come to understand and maybe believe that the man who does it is somehow imbued with great kindness and wisdom, that, somehow, the pipeman knows something other than the obvious. This would be special if it were true. I don't see it, though, in others or in myself. Maybe I'm smoking the wrong tobacco, have yet to select the correct pipe, or am oblivious to a certain trick. Once I thought I wasn't trying hard enough, so I smoked and smoked all day and managed eight pipes before I gave it up. The only wisdom I gained that day was to never do it again. And I often fret about not being kind enough to others or to my pets. I find it hard to be kind day in day out. Animals are pretty easy because they keep coming back for as much abuse as you can dish out. But people can be trouble. I really do try to be a good fellow, but I often discern the other guy just ain't worthy. Doesn't he know that the pipeman is his ace in the hole? You know what they say about no good deed going unpunished. But I'm no quitter, so I keep at it, hoping.

Perhaps you'll be better at it than me and fit the nostalgic image of the pipe smoker truer to his mythical form.

I think it's an age thing. At some point, as you traverse through life, you give up trying to prove yourself. You slow down and are okay with letting civilization get on without you; but this is for the old, not the youthful. I haven't given up the ship yet. When I do—if I do—I suppose I will have gained that air of kindness and wisdom that I'm supposed to have as a pipeman. Time will tell. I'm no model pipeman, mind you. I think that smoking a pipe necessarily slows you down so that you can proceed a little more thoughtfully.

2

The *Real* Pipeman is Dead

pipeman— *n*. **1.** A man who smokes tobacco in a pipe; principally of the heath-briar type but also from the calabash, clay, corncob and meerschaum. **2.** An older man, generally, from any walk of life, who smokes his pipe regularly in his daily activities. **3.** A person who collects pipes for hobby. **4.** During the period 1850–1950, a gentleman who regaled himself as a connoisseur in the art of smoking, enjoying the use of its associative appurtenances, including the smoking room, smoking cap and jacket, tobacco jars and humidors, and the pleasure taken from the slow process of coloring an expertly carved figural meerschaum pipe through its smoking.

—Anonymous

MAYBE you should smoke a cigar. Cigars are alive and well. Big machers smoke 'em, and why shouldn't you act like one? I'll tell you why: Generally, cigar smokers are not big shots; they may act like it when they're surrounded by their cigar-smoking pals, but most are plain souls just like you looking for solace in an historically American pastime. You should not smoke a cigar because Arnold smokes 'em. Nor because a friend thinks he's being kind by giving you a Cuban at your office Christmas party. You should smoke a cigar because you'll generally avert the quizzical looks brought on by smoking a pipe. And because it just seems to be you. They're easier to smoke than pipes, much easier. They're sexier to women—or men, as the case may be, the metro-sexual or the full-blown variety. And, most important, the cigar is au courant. "But, of course, we must cut our coat according to our cloth. One of the saddest things in life ... is that the most refined men are often hampered by limited incomes. Or, to put it in a more concrete form, many a man who is worthy of the finest Magnifico Pomposos is obliged to put up with 'Dutchmen,' twopenny cheroots, or Burmah cigars" (Expert Wrinkler, "Hints on Smoking," *Punch*, [London: Vol. CXXVI January–June 1904, March 9], 178).   The one thing the pipe has over the cigar is that puff per puff the pipe offers better value, particularly if your intent is to smoke quality tobacco, whether rolled into a stick or shredded and pressed into the bowl.   Mon ami, the choice is yours. But if for some mysterious reason the

"… and then take shooting. After all, Sir, isn't it rather primitive to want to shoot things?"

thought of the pipe has you in its sights, then read on, 'cause this book is for you.

The decision on what to smoke is not entirely yours. You see, history has something to say about your choice. You may think that you'll make the ideal pipeman. Chances are you probably won't. Pipes demand a certain type and, as you are by now acutely aware by the few smoking them, many have not passed the grade. Cigarmen rarely smoke a pipe. Zino Davidoff, *the* legendary cigarman would usually smoke a pipe at home, but you're no Zino; so make your choice here and now: cigar or pipe. The pipeman will occasionally cross over and dabble in a choice Dominican, Honduran, or Nicaraguan, but he'll know where he's most comfortable and come home to his pipe.

Sometimes a pipe is more than a cigar. Zino Davidoff (1906–1994) knew. Here, he lights up a briar in the Canadian shape.

Courtesy Davidoff

Read the history of the pipeman. Turn off the television and your Internet browser and go to the library. No, don't do that, because puritanical library boards de-accessioned books having anything to do with tobacco and the lowly vice of smoking. If that inexplicable grip of life is truly leading you to the pipe then you'll need to look elsewhere for the age-old story of the pipeman. He has been written about for centuries, but you'll need to mine hard and smart to find the right titles, but they do exist. Are you up to the task? (I've made it trouble-free for you by including a recommended reading list in chapter 4.)

When you get started with your reading assignment you'll slowly begin to understand about the real pipeman—while he may not be completely relegated to the past, he is a shadow—a wisp?—of his former self. If after trudging through several titles you remain undeterred in your quest to become a pipeman, there may be hope and a gap for you to enter the cadre of those worthy enough to enjoy the pleasures and respect the pipe bestows.

Those few souls you see about town and country puffing away effortlessly on their pipe are, broadly speaking, real pipemen. Not, mind you, the pipeman of yesteryear, the classic pipeman, but the modern-day pipeman, and that's who you will be and who I shall mold you into becoming.

The pipeman of days gone by lived by a different tune. Smoke was everywhere, and no one gave it much thought. The pipe was as much a benign appendage as it was a much-loved device delivering not only a wholesome smoke, but also a manly aura that, well, others admired. The pipeman was not ostentatious; smoking a pipe was something done with aplomb, and it was as natural a motion as breathing and walking. He *was* the pipe.

VIRGINIA TOBACCO.

Two maiden dames of sixty-two
Together long had dwelt:
Neither, alas! of love so true,
The bitter pangs had felt.

But age comes on, they say, apace,
To warn us of our death,
And wrinkles mar the fairest face,
At last it stops our breath.

One of these dames, tormented sore
With that curst pang, a tooth-ache,
Was at a loss for such a bore
What remedy to take:

"I've heard," thought she, "this ill to cure,
A pipe is good, they say,
Well then, tobacco I'll endure,
And smoke the pain away."

The pipe was lit, the tooth soon well,
And she retir'd to rest—
When thus the other ancient belle
Her spinster mate addressed:—

"Let me request a favour, pray"—
"I'll do it if I can"—
"Oh! well then, love, smoke every day,
You smell so like a man! " [*]

(John Stanley Gregson, *Gimcrackiana*, 1833)

Today's pipeman has a substantially different tune to live by; he's had to adapt to get by. Of course, many could not, and that's why the pipe evolved into the strange bird that it is. He is rarely permitted to smoke in public, and most find him quite distasteful. (The same is true for the cigar, but much less so. Still there are restaurants that permit the cigar, but not the pipe. What little they know!)

Nowadays, the pipeman is not expected, nor is it possible, to live in a cloud of constant smoke as his forebears once did. It is enough to smoke in the quiet, private moments, enjoying a national pastime, albeit an historic relic of the past, practicing its gentle art fittingly and, above all else, living for the moment of the next pipe.

Do you still remain steadfast in becoming today's pipeman? I hope so. In time, and it will take years, you'll come to find that not only will you derive more pleasure from the pipe than the cigar (forgive me, Zino), but you'll be incredulous as to how you've been able to survive for so many years without it. Onward ho!

---

[*] Walter Hamilton, *Parodies of the Works of English and American Authors*, vol. 6, (London: Reeves & Turner, 1889), 148.

3

What to Do if You're New

Many are called but few are chosen. Most people remain at this juvenile, cigarette-smoking level. Others advance, after some hesitancy, to the stage of cigar-smoking. But only relatively few are swayed by the sacred unrest leading to progress and perfection. After long and arduous struggles, these courageous persons have realised that nothing equals the joy of holding a pipe in one's mouth, sitting in a comfortable chair and gazing peacefully at the mighty stream of life.

—Joaquin Verdaguer, *The Art of Pipe Smoking*

WHEN I travel light in the wilderness by wood and canvas canoe, pack and wannigan, I will occasionally sight another tripper across a lake or river. I can tell a lot by how he paddles, how his canoe meanders on the water, the silhouette of the boat and other nuances that would give away who he is and the experience he packs beneath his tumpline. The same can be said of the pipeman. He may see him coming across a room, sitting on a park bench or at a gathering of hobbyists at a pipe show. The taking of a pipe is a rather nuanced affair. To the novice eye, the pipe smoker will be engaged in the obvious, smoking. But to the observant pipeman, a multitude of actions and motions are taking place, many simultaneously. As a raw cadet to the pipe you will believe that its mastery is attainable with some degree of ease. Perhaps you got started with a pipe, say five years ago, and that you've mastered what it is. On both accounts you'd be wrong.

(This chapter is a launching point for many of the ideas dedicated to their own chapter later in the book. The ideas will be broached now for those too impatient to take in the full primer.)

If you take away and forever remember one small thing from this book, it should be this: there is no greater self-pleasure in life than the mastery of a practice. And I unquestionably include the taking of a pipe as such a worthy practice to seek the mastery of. In the several hours it will take you to read this book you will begin to realize that there's much more to the pipe than merely smoking it. This disquisition goes beyond the commonplace and pedantic; it delves deep into your responsibilities to yourself, the tradition of pipe smoking, because you are choosing to become one of its peers, and to those you interact with in daily life, of which the pipe will hopefully be your expected and trustworthy companion.

Sacred is the pipe. Long before your trivial presence graced the earth, the Indian of the plains was smoking a pipe, a calumet of red pipestone and reed, bequeathed to him by the Master of Life, Gitche Manito. I suppose Henry Wadsworth Longfellow was there because he wrote about it in the *Song of Hiawatha*:

> Bathe now in the stream before you,
> Wash the war-paint from your faces,
> Wash the blood-stains from your fingers,
> Bury your war-clubs and your weapons,
> Break the red stone from this quarry,
> Mould and make it into Peace-Pipes,
> Take the reeds that grow beside you,
> Deck them with your brightest feathers,
> Smoke the calumet together,
> And as brothers live henceforward!

(lines 124–133)

As fictional and as Victorian-romantic as *Hiawatha* may have been, its foundation was deeply rooted in Indian belief and practice. The pipe and smoking were sacrosanct. Well, that was then. In this 21st century we have other aggravations in life to confront on a daily basis; and like the trusted companion that it is, your pipe is there for you. For this reason the pipe remains true to the ages as the great consoler.

Let's go

Okay, so I'm going to assume you already have a pipe and purchased tobacco someone told you was delectable. This is not the way you should be starting out, but it's the time-honored way, so I guess it would be considered sacrilegious any other way; and, at the very least, you'll have one more trifling horror story to add to your biography. Save yourself some embarrassment and steal yourself away to a hidden spot where no will see you, because anyone who takes the pipe for the first time looks like an idiot. Now, jam the tobacco into the pipe's bowl and let the fire burn!

So, how was the experience? Great, huh? Be honest now. It was just horrible, wasn't it? You say that if this is what pipe smoking is, then you'll have none of it. No wonder all the pipemen are dead; their pipes killed them! So now what are you going to do?

The British Character. Love of Pipe-Smoking.

At this juncture, with the whole of your mouth seemingly burnt, you just don't see the point to enduring the torture. Perhaps you're right. If your life has been marked by quitting whenever things looked their bleakest, then yes, quit. Why change your life mid-stream? This Bud's not for you.

But if you're not of that loathsome quitting ilk, listen up. Here's what I want you to do: throw away that *delectable* tobacco; for now hold onto the pipe, though in time you'll wonder what possessed you to purchase it; apply ass to chair, and continue reading this book to its conclusion. What you've just learned in your first miserable pipe-smoking experience, is the pipe can be a rascally beast of a cauldron. And, like every pipeman before you, you stepped up and passed the first test—survived may be a more fitting statement of the ordeal. But at this point you're well on your way to becoming a pipeman. All the rest will be downhill.

The tobacconist

You may have to interrupt this pipe thing for a while and get on with life, so this book will have to wait. And between now and then, you may be thinking of visiting that smoke shop you've known of all these years but never had the need to visit. Alright, go, but don't buy a bloody thing—you're not ready yet.

Whatever the shop is called—Cheap Smokes, Discount Cigarettes, Sherlock's Emporium, Tinder Box, and the like—it won't be the shop for you, at least not yet. Unless you're able to distinguish the wheat from the chaff, and you're not, be wary as you enter the merchant's domain. For all intents and purposes, that romantic version you may have of the traditional tobacconist no longer exists. Smoking styles have changed; modern-day puritanical society has cast a pall over the whole notion of tobacco use; state excise taxation is beyond the pale; and Internet shopping has cheapened what once was a tidy industry where knowledgeable tobacconists plied a trade that was honorable, and where one could be counseled correctly in what to do and what to buy. Then, you could establish a relationship with a clerk you could rely on for all your smoking requisites.

These days, the smoke shop in your town or just off the highway in that strip mall will carry all the manly necessities, including—mostly—cigarettes and RYO (roll-your-own), cigars, glass crack pipes, marijuana bongs, a wide assortment of Chinese lighters, and other such similarly injection-molded crap, samurai swords, air guns, energy drinks, candy bars, Fritos and Doritos, maybe beer and, oftentimes, low-end dildos and vibrators. The shopkeep, who, nowadays, and for no apparent reason, will be a first- or second-generation immigrant from South Asia—will know little about his product line other than its markup and that it is the best of its kind. Suspect everything this man or his wife or mother or son or grandmother tells you; they know nothing about the pipe even though they will have a small assortment. So, unless your wife makes a special, amorous request of you late one evening, you'll know better than to shop at these joints ever again.

Not all smoke shops are as pathetic but, sadly, most are. You might not have much better in your town. Consider a move to the big city. But every now and then a shop of promise will be close at hand. You may have been in the shop before, but then you knew nothing, so it made little or no impression on you. This book, however, will begin to broaden your vision to some interesting possibilities.

You say, "Now this looks like a real tobacconist!" It says tobacconist on the sign, so it must be. Maybe. You walk in and there they are, pipes. They're everywhere: on the wall, in glass cabinets, and in the window. There are also lots of glass jars full of tobacco. At the rear of the store, or alongside a wall with a sliding door, will be the cigar humidor. The remainder of the store, perhaps half its contents, will be comprised of crap similar to that other smoke shop you visited previously, but this shop's crap is of superior quality. Remember rule number one, buy nothing—you're there just to observe and to soak it all in.

This will be a hard thing for you to do. The clerk behind the counter will eventually discover, through friendly discourse, that you're a greenhorn and will try to set you up with a starter kit—another budding pipeman killer if ever there was. And heavens, do not waltz into the store with your lover in tow. She will be impatient and either urge you to drop the ridiculous notion of becoming a pipeman or wheedle you into listening to the clerk so you can move on to more interesting shopping grounds at the mall. Oy. If you're not already of age, trust me when I tell you that the relationship will prosper, but only if you shop alone. As far as pipe smoking goes, women are there to enjoy in your pleasure and little else. A sexist remark it is not, just fact. Rare is it for the fairer sex to partake in the pipe.

So you think this shop has potential, do you? Here, too, the man behind the counter should be looked on with no small modicum of circumspection. Unless he's the owner of the shop, what he may or may not know, you will not be able to deduce at this stage, but taking his advice on that starter kit will almost assuredly end in another bad experience.

Why is this so? The man works as a tobacconist, does he not? No, never make such an assumption. Operating the register does not a tobacconist make! That won't stop the employee from confidently selecting the most popular and flavorful tobacco, an entry-level pipe in the $19.95 to $29.95 range, some pipe cleaners, a tobacco tamper and, perhaps, he'll toss in a Bic lighter gratis, you being a new customer and all. Don't take the shopkeep's assurances as sensible experience.

I'll tell you, it's a real shame that this goes on, day in and day out, at most shops across the country. Employees are expected to learn on the job, and most get it wrong in the beginning and perpetuate the lesson as inferior advice to the customer, doing his employer a great disservice. There was a time in this country when the trades were looked on with pride; now there's only contempt. There's this perception of family shame if little Johnny can't quite make a go of it at university. The trades are not a dead-end! Western Europe has proved this to the detriment of the United States. Currently, there is a shortage of highly skilled workers of the blue-collar type. And, yes, often times those skilled hands make wages similar to those of their college graduate brethren when and where market demand is hot.

Retail shops were no different. New hires apprenticed. They were not permitted to sell to the customer until management felt they had attained sufficient knowledge of its wares and expertise in salesmanship. Today, it's appalling what many establishments refer to as service, even at high-profile chains. Customer service means returns and exchanges—a regrettable experience. So pity the tobacconist's clerk and caveat emptor!

Your first learned purchase

You will buy this: a straight billiard-shaped briar pipe, a medium-strength English tobacco mixture, and a $1 pipe tamper (looks like a horseshoe nail). And don't forget to help yourself to several boxes of wooden safety matches most tobacconists of repute offer their clients. Why all this?

For the pipe, trust me on this. In time, and after trying many styles and shapes of briar, you'll come back to the straight billiard or one of its variants, like the Canadian, Liverpool, or Lovat—most do. (Especially the Canadian because there's more wood in the shank than vulcanite, and wood is nicer to look at while vulcanite deteriorates; the acrylic/plastic mouthpieces are, well, plastic.) If your pocketbook can afford it, go for an English-made brand. No country since the practice of turning pipes on a lathe began in the latter half of the 19th century, has produced a finer pipe than the British manufactories. Expect to pay from $65 to $125, a tidy sum, but a sound investment on the pleasures to follow. Look around and get one sized not too small and not too big. The billiard is the most refined and elegant-shaped pipe and, functionally, one of the driest pipes to smoke.

When you've found a pipe that appears suitable, have the clerk put it aside momentarily. Ask him if he carries used pipes. Yes, they are a commodity worthy of your scrutiny. The shop may advertise them as estate pipes. These pipes, whatever their origin, if well cared for by the previous owner(s), will offer you tremendous value. To boot, it's broken-in and will, in all likelihood, immediately launch you into that type of good smoke reserved exclusively for the knowledgeable pipeman. Many a new pipe—and you'll have trouble telling which ones—can take several bowls of tobacco before being broken-in and smoking yummy. Ask the clerk to demonstrate to you that the pipe is clean—in the argot of the hobby, "rejuvenated"—and has no faults. Oftentimes, you'll be able to score a fine Ashton, Charatan, Comoy, Dunhill, GBD, Sasieni, or other classic English-brand pipe this way. Expect to pay no more than $150.

As to your weed of choice, again, also English. But in tobacco, English refers to a type as opposed to a country of manufacture, though it did begin in the Isles for sure. With the release of the first edition of *Confessions*, Dunhill's My Mixture 965 was the recommended tobacco for the nascent pipeman, and the benchmark against which all other Full English mixtures were compared. Still is. But only as recent memory permits as 965 is no longer exported to North America from Denmark where it is made by the Orlik Company. Dunhill 965 didn't win praise from your wife because to those accustomed to the aroma of sweet-smelling tobacco mixtures, such as cherry Cavendish, vanilla nougat, peach melba, or rum, a classic English is the antithesis. But you smoke for you, not for them, so smoke English! (Perhaps I am too rigid and unrealistic in this last bit of direction. Prudence may very well indicate that if you value a warm and dry place to eat, smoke, and sleep, you may have to revise your choice of tobaccos so that a favorable room aroma is established, at least some of the time.) Quality English mixtures, like Dunhill's, smoked dry as opposed to wet, like the sweet tobaccos you first experimented with that burnt your mouth. A dry-burning tobacco in a dry-smoking pipe will give you immense pleasure.

The loss of 965 was catastrophic to pipemen who had made it their standard mixture, especially to ones who had not inventoried it sufficiently. It is too soon to tell if the void on the throne of the Full English mixture will ever be filled again. Frankly, at the time of writing of this second edition, I myself am in between many fine Full English mixtures, yet am hesitant to recommend any one English or Balkan mixture.

But I am prepared to recommend the mark of G.L. Pease. Pease is one of the best-known blenders in the States these past 12 years and mixes up some of the most luxe English mixtures. Look for any of his English or Balkan mixtures, notably Charring Cross, Odyssey, and Westminster. Know this: if the shop you're in carries Pease, it's no slouch. Otherwise, go to the Web and get this stuff. And while Pease has nowhere near the merchandise history of Dunhill, frankly, the mixtures are at least available and at a reasonable cost.

I told you in the beginning that I would not get bogged down in the intricacies of packing, lighting and smoking, as it relates to your satisfaction and, if you will, the mechanics behind the tiny combustion chamber where it all happens. This is truly a gradual learning process that will take years to get just right so that maximum enjoyment is derived from smoking what is, today, a costly tobacco. I know this sounds absurd to you right now, but trust me that it is what it is. Other books, like those I've recommended for you to acquire and read from the list in chapter 4, cover the bowl packing and lighting process well enough.

Just this, though: if you do one thing right from the get-go, pack the tobacco in the bowl not too densely and not too loosely either, just enough so there's a small amount of spring. Remember, air is needed for the combustion process. Restrict the air and you'll burn through too many matches and have yourself another case of burnt tongue. Too dense and you'll be sucking beyond good measure, literally and figuratively. Ask your new tobacconist friend to assist you in this regard.

Before you leave the shop, ask the clerk if he is aware of a local pipe club and where and when it meets. If one does exist close by, at all costs, you must go to it. There you will be among friends. Today the club is a very safe harbor for the pipeman that you have launched yourself into becoming.

A note to the tobacconist

It's not all your fault. You've had a difficult time of it, what with excessive excise taxes applied by your state government; pipemen who no longer stop by the shop, because they had the nerve to die with no proper notice; society frowns on any form of smoking, because cigarette smokers are fools, over do things, and have made a miserable mess for pipe smokers having to live under the oppressive anti-smoking movement; and there is the Internet, where pipemen can buy things without your knowledge or benefit.

What to do? Do you want to continue being a tobacconist, or just look at finding things—anything—that you can sell in the shop to keep afloat? Well, if you have little to no interest in retraining to become a barista selling tall, decaf lattés, ceramic figurines, or such other similar schlock, then here are two bits of advice.

First, get into secondhand pipes real big. Some shops have been doing it for years and are able to attract the Internet-collector crowd who seek out the old, tired, and often rejuvenated briar. Today's pipeman who knows what's what is looking for the classic stuff the English firms—what's left of them— aren't making anymore, save Dunhill, some would argue.

Second, get to know what your clerks know and don't know—test them. They'll never know all that you know, but they need to have more than a working knowledge of the trade to keep the till ringing. I suggest that any current or new hires be made to read three books, and for them to be tested on their comprehension of the material: Richard Hacker's *The Ultimate Pipe Book*, Robert F. Winans's *The Pipe Smoker's Tobacco Book*, and Carl Ehwa Jr.'s *The Book of Pipes & Tobacco*. You may not care for Hacker's magnum opus, but I think his work remains one of the hobby's best all-rounders on the subject. Prepare a test from each book. If the clerk passes, he keeps his job. But you're not done yet. Don't think for a minute that because the lad passed his tests he knows a lick about selling. He should be made to pass similar basic tests in the art of retail salesmanship. Find your own books on the subject and test him again. Keep testing the lad, giving him the opportunity to make more money on each sale. Keep him happy: he'll remain loyal to you, will never steal from you, and your customers will keep coming back wanting to buy only from the lad.

Finally, have a presence on the Web. The overhead will be close to nil, and you'll create a much larger secondary market distinct from your primary walk-in traffic. The lad probably knows all about it, so volunteer him to be your Webmaster.

About public smoking, its death may be overly exaggerated, but not by much. If you plan on remaining solvent and keeping up the good fight, it's you or the Internet. Not only can you compete, but you can use it to your advantage. Get current, get smart, and you'll do all right. And by all means, consider starting an after-hours pipe club at the shop.

4

Reading the Lifestyle

When a subject becomes totally obsolete we make it a required course.

—Peter Drucker

T HE pipeman should own more books than pipes. If you're contemplating building a pipe collection or, if you're already a seasoned collector of briars, clays, meerschaums, or tins of vintage tobacco, put your hoarding instinct—which you may have confused with collecting—on pause and switch to books. While pipe smoking is seemingly an obsolete pastime, I doubt Peter Drucker's observation will ever come to fruition. In fact, centuries ago in England the proper way to smoke tobacco in a pipe was taught to school boys, it was thought, the use of tobacco would prevent and drive away all manners of illnesses. Today, of course, the opposite is thought to be true. Look, this book will end soon and then what will you do? Regardless of your tenure with the pipe, your best investment is in you. Nurture your interests and feed your mind with knowledge from reading books. As it relates to your education on becoming a pipeman or a better pipeman, as the case may be, books will deliver to you lessons that cannot be casually absorbed by visiting your tobacconist, pipe show or the typical pipe club meeting; frankly, most pipe smokers consider themselves well-versed in the pipe, but that is merely one aspect that today's classic pipeman must be conversant in.

Taking up the pipe should signify that you've adopted a certain lifestyle. And that lifestyle must include a penchant for daily reading. You can do it, but first you must turn off all your digital information screens, because the best reading is not on the Internet or in your TV Guide, but between the covers of books and journals. Read what you will, but don't narrow your focus such that all you can natter on about at cocktail parties is the state of the Detroit auto industry. So even though you're a gear-head, remember that you're also a pipeman, and there are expectations of you, like knowing something more than about your pipe's unusual shape or that you like such and such a tobacco. For heaven's sake, know of what you do!

Sad to say, these days the bookworm is about as much an anachronism as the pipeman. "We are going down to a gulag archipelago of readers. Of the sort of readers I've described, there are 176 of them in Nashville, 432 in Atlanta, 4011 in Chicago, 3017 in Los Angeles and 7000 in New York. It adds up to 60,000 people. I assure you there are no more" (Philip Roth cited in Esther B. Fein, 'Philip Roth Sees Double. And Maybe Triple, Too,' *New York Times*, March 9, 1993). Everyone has their face glued to their screen, and, frankly, not enjoying it a whole lot. (I mean, how much Internet porn can one man consume in a weekend anyway? Okay, some tastes are insatiable, but you need balance in your life.) Besides, there's no better time to read than when you're smoking, because both endeavors are carried out mostly in the sitting position. And reading about pipes and smoking history is something you'll find to be rather enjoyable while smoking your pipe in your favorite armchair.

What you'll get from reading about this ancient pastime of smoking, apart from the in-the-moment pleasure, is a broadening of your perspective of everything that happened *before you* (somewhat akin to Before Christ, but without the capitalization). It's all there, mostly good, though mostly anti-smoking since the 1980s. By reading, you'll become aware of what is expected of you, and what you'll surely take to as a fish takes to water. You must not fail yourself in this aspect of your upbringing, because before you most have. Take this route to becoming the quintessential pipeman in the classical sense.

The author inscribing a copy of his first book for a pipe-smoking reader.

So, what to read? Here's my reading list for you. Get every one, and in any order. There will be others you will come across, but these are the essentials that every pipeman worth his dottle must have in his smoking library:

Apperson, G.L. I.S.O. *The Social History of Smoking*. London, England: Martin Secker, 1914

Bain, John. *Tobacco in Song & Story*. New York, NY: H. M. Caldwell Co., 1896

Barrie, J.M. *My Lady Nicotine*. London, England: Hodder and Stoughton, 1890

Crowquill, Alfred. *A Few Words About Pipes, Smoking & Tobacco*. New York, NY: New York Public Library, Arents Tobacco Collection, 1947

Davidoff, Zino. *The Connoisseur's Book of The Cigar*. New York, NY: McGraw-Hill, 1969

Dunhill, Alfred. *The Pipe Book*. London, England: A & C Black, Ltd., 1924

————, **Alfred H**. *The Gentle Art of Smoking*. London, England: Max Reinhardt, 1954

————, **Mary**. *Our Family Business*. London, England: The Bodley Head, 1979

Ehwa, Carl, Jr. *The Book of Pipes & Tobaccos*. New York, NY: Random House, 1974

Fairholt, F.W., F.S.A. *Tobacco: Its History & Associations: Including An Account Of The Plant And Its Manufacture: With Its Mode Of Use In All Ages And Countries*. London, England: Chatto and Windus, 1859; and 2nd edition, 1876

Hacker, Richard Carlton. *The Ultimate Pipe Book*. Beverly Hills, CA: Autumn Gold Publ., 1997

Herment, Georges. *The Pipe*. London, England: Cassell & Co. Ltd., 1954

Hilton, Matthew. *Smoking in Popular British Culture 1800–2000*. Manchester, England: Manchester University Press, 2000

Jahn, Raymond. *Tobacco Dictionary*. New York, NY: Philosophical Library, 1954

James I. *A Counter-Blaste to Tobacco*. London, England: The Rodale Press, 1954

Knight, Joseph. *Pipe and Pouch: The Smokers Own Book of Poetry*. Boston, MA: Joseph Knight Co., 1895

Liebaert, Alexis and Maya, Alain. *The Illustrated History of The Pipe*. Suffolk, England: Harold Stark Publishers Ltd, 1994

Newcombe, Rick. *In Search of Pipe Dreams*. Los Angeles, CA: Sumner Books, 2003

Ram, Sidney P. *How to Get More Fun Out of Smoking*. Chicago, IL: Cuneo Press, 1941

Rapaport, Ben. *The Complete Guide to Collecting Antique Pipes*. Exton, PA: Schiffer Publishing Ltd., 1979

————. *Collecting Antique Meerschaums: Miniature to Majestic Sculpture, 1850–1925*. Atglen, PA: Schiffer Publishing Ltd., 1999

Schmidt, Jacek. *The Pipe's Rebirth: Production, Maintenance and Restoration*. Poland: privately printed, 2005

Schnitzer, Raymond J. *Leaves From A Tobaccoman's Log*. New York, NY: Vantage Press, 1970

Schrier, Gary B. *The History of The Calabash Pipe*. Seattle, WA: privately printed, 2006

Sherman, Milton M. *All About Tobacco*. New York, NY: Sherman National Corp., 1970

Stokkebye, Peter. *The Life & Good Times of a Tobacco Man*. Corral de Tierra, CA: Selective American Marketing, 2002

Verdaguer, Joaquin. *The Art of Pipe Smoking*. London, England: Curlew Press Limited, 1958

Weber, Carl. *The Pleasures of Pipe Smoking*. New York, NY: Thomas Nelson & Sons, 1965

————. *Weber's Guide to Pipes and Pipe Smoking*. New York, NY: Cornerstone Library, 1962

Winans, Robert F. *The Pipe Smoker's Tobacco Book*. Provincetown, MA: Privately Printed, 1977

Note: Many of these citations are available as reprints, few as later editions.

Where will you acquire these books? Needless to say, virtually all of the books on this list are long out-of-print. (You'll have to turn on one of your screens for this next part.) The Internet has several excellent bookseller search engines to assist. (My favorite online book store is www.alibris.com.) And you should investigate the site Google Book Search. With Google's plan to optically scan every book ever published, many of the older tomes in the public domain—and many that are not—are available for viewing free of charge. It's stunning the amount of recent and long-forgotten pipe history which one can access with scarcely the tap of a finger at the keyboard.

Now, if you're old-school and like the human touch, there is but one antiquarian bookseller stateside who has been specializing in tobacco titles for 40 years and will be energetic in communicating with you by both email and snail-mail in filling your requests. Ben Rapaport is the man and his quarterly newsletter and stock list of available titles is called the *Nicotian Network and Nexus*. Subscription to the list is free as long as you make the occasional purchase. His prices are fair and service is quick. But make no mistake at believing a resource such as this will be around whenever you're ready to commit to real pipe-learning. Ben is a crank of the finest kind to those who show they are worthy of his time and energy. He keeps threatening to fold his table and move on, because he feels people are more inclined to spend $500 on a pipe than $50 on a book. Start your library now! (Contact Ben Rapaport at ben70gray@gmail.com or 9831 Highland Glen Place, Colorado Springs, CO 80920.)

Aside from books, there are two magazines currently in print that are worthy of your attention. The first is the *Pipe Collector*, which is the organ of the North American Society of Pipe Collectors, a group of some 1,000 souls who can't get enough from every issue. Its editor is a swell, PhD-toting pipeman by the name of Bill Unger who, bless his self-effacing style, compiles material for each issue, rather than edit in the classic sense of the profession (much like that other generous sole who founded and edited the *Pipe Smoker's Ephemeris*, the late Tom Dunn). The *Pipe Collector* is more of a newsletter than a magazine; is B&W; contains almost no adverts; and, best of all, is negligible in cost for the six bi-monthly issues. But the content is sound, with written submissions contributed exclusively by its members who, while generally quite knowledgeable and pipemen through and through, can and do sometimes have very strong beliefs on matters both trivial and some less so (tempers do flare on occasion). Its content is, for the most part, quotidian, with much historical conjecture on pipe- and tobacco-makers. Subscribe for as long as you can stand it. (Visit the society online at www.naspc@naspc.org; write to them at P.O. Box 9642, Columbus, OH, 43209-9642.)

The other magazine of the hobby is *Pipes and Tobaccos*. As production goes, it's the antithesis of the *Pipe Collector*. It's been around for 15 years; has an average readership base of 6,200; is four-color glossy; has a stable of professional writers; advertising is present in too small a quantity (Good you say? I say not!); is a quarterly; and the cost is reasonable. Back issues through its first issue in 1996 are easily obtainable through the magazine or online and would be a sound addition to the library you will build.

Though the production is first-rate, for better or worse, the magazine is one-dimensional; that is, pipes and tobaccos are all that's written about. Like a typical hobby rag, it keeps to what it knows and believes its readers want, no more. Let's call it focused. Depending on your perspective, this may or may not be an off-putting or limiting objective. Conversely, the magazine for the cigarman, *Cigar Aficionado*, sees its mission quite differently. While the cigar is its primary focus, the editorial passion and, indeed, vision, are broader. *Aficionado* sees the cigar lover as having a life beyond or intertwined with his "smoke," and so it caters with stories and complementary advertisements for the finer things in life—as they see them—from golf and travel destinations, to fine dining and luxury trappings—most unattainable to the bulk of its readership, I postulate. The magazine has a very real touch of *Esquire*, *GQ*, and *Men's Vogue*.

If *Pipes and Tobaccos* stays focused solely on the hobby, rather than offering coverage of the broader lifestyle issues and events of today's pipe smokers, then its current format, more or less, suffices. However, if its subscriber population dwindles, the editor and publisher may have to freshen its business model, acknowledging that the pipeman, like his counterpart, the cigarman, has other needs and desires beyond the smokeables that ought to be found in print journalism.

The author at Chicagoland 2010 with his historical compilation on Loewe, the first-ever study of this once great English pipe-making firm. It was the final part of a trilogy of the great English pipe catalogues of the early 20th century that includes BBB and Dunhill.

(Since the first edition of *Confessions*, the average readership base has, indeed, dwindled from 10,000 to 6,200.)

On second thought, "more or less" and "suffices," are not good enough! I know from having spoken with its editor, Chuck Stanion, a few years ago, the magazine is keen on keeping fresh for a contented and burgeoning readership. But, to this subscriber, few material and substantive—only cosmetic—changes have been made to it in the past few years. This is unfortunate, because opportunities to do so abound.

For instance, many pipemen belong to clubs, and they were dealt a blow a while back when the page that listed regional clubs was relocated from the back of the magazine to its website. *P&T*'s most ardent supporters are the same people who are active in their local clubs. The magazine should expand its coverage beyond just listing addresses. It should report on various club activities, because clubs are where the hobby is alive and well!

Another example of where *P&T* can broaden its coverage is by a more concerted effort to cover the national and large regional shows. For the pipemen who have not yet attended such a show, especially the springtime Chicagoland show and autumnal CORPS show in Richmond, Virginia, the "who's who" of Smokedom flock there; they're the pipemen's Capistrano! Oh the colorful characters and the spontaneous stories to be recounted would fill many pages of every quarterly issue, but *P&T* gives but scant coverage to these Meccas for smokers and collectors who come from near and far. But you must know this is not an editorial oversight. Time and again, Stanion has commiserated with me that it boils down to the all consuming advertising dollar; and in the land of pipe smoking, there's very little of it about.

And, perhaps, very painfully for me, it is strange that *P&T* opts not to review new books on pipes and tobacco … yet pertinent and relevant literature is the grist that expands our knowledge base. Just about every magazine, newspaper, and journal devotes a column to review new books, but *P&T* does not. I queried the editor on why, and he responded that nothing is gained if, perchance, the magazine's review of a book is highly critical. In my view, an objective book review rendered by a knowledgeable authority reveals to the prospective buyer the merits—or lack thereof—of a new work. "Authors must be made accountable for their thinking. Their ideas should be interrogated, their thoughts dissected, their prose criticized, their sources closely examined, their evidence scrutinized for some semblance to fact" (Sherman Young, *The Book is Dead: Long Live the Book*, [Sydney: University of New South Wales Press, 2007], 110). If the critique is negative, it should not be viewed as a personal attack on the author; it is a professional evaluation, a cautionary note for the greater good of the reading public. Moreover, the magazine should realize that it is selling stories. That it chooses not to be a sounding board for non-competing literary works is a business model that is intellectually deficient and myopic. I would argue: embrace the written word! Isn't this what

P&T is striving to achieve with its publication targeted on a shrinking population of pipemen?

All is not lost, it seems, because with the winter 2010 issue the editorial staff of the magazine finally decided to review a book, but what a book: *Velvet Glove, Iron Fist, A History of Anti-Smoking* by Christopher Snowdon. I've not read the title, but from the review it is most assuredly a story which everyone knows about; one that nobody likes; and of the deceitful, conniving, puritanical movement that so threatens the livelihood of the pipeman. It was a sour note upon which to end the issue. By history, of course, the topic is centered largely upon the cigarette. And if there is one thing that has done more to extinguish the pipeman's love affair with his briar it is the false association that the pipe has to cigarettes. I hope on the next go round, the editorial staff selects a more palatable book.

To its credit, the magazine does announce new releases in Pipe Stuff, the new product showcase, a gratis gesture, but this is no substitute for reporting more fully on the latest pipe or tobacco book. After all, in our present-day, dreadful, anti-smoking landscape, so few new books are published, they all certainly deserve our attention. Pipemen read, maybe not as much as before the era of digital media, but many still enjoy the printed word.

The content of the Internet is ephemeral: you never can tell how long a page will be listed or moved, never to be found again, Google notwithstanding. The pipeman is a tactile being; a "work" needs to be held, seen, or waiting patiently on bookshelf, desk, or table. He should not be satisfied solely with the Internet. Must he be relegated to enjoying his pipe while seated and staring at a computer screen? This ambiance cannot match the clarity of the printed page or the comfort of a favorite chair in which he can lazily slouch. For him, the new pipe or tobacco book is hope eternal that smoking, one of the cherished foundations of his lifestyle, will continue on for yet a few more years. When will *P&T* get it right and freshen up?

But is it possible for the magazine to reform itself? Truth be told, today, there are fewer pipe or tobacco firms of material substance able to support such a broader focus (read more magazine pages). And ad budgets are what makes or breaks it for any magazine. But the problem lies deeper than this: there is no critical mass of pipemen. And of those few remaining puffers of the noble briar, they're not seen by those same advertisers that spend regularly at *Aficionado* as cigar smokers. And cigarmen there are aplenty.

When considering economic viability, reflect on this market barometer. Publishing house Penguin Group considers cigar-smokers idiots, but apparently the editorial board is correct in its conviction that many of them would have an interest and the ability to read about cigars, because its book, the *Complete Idiot's Guide to* Cigars, by Tad Gage, is in its second edition (no small feat in the world of publishing, I can assure you). I would bet Penguin thought for two seconds on doing such a guide book on pipes before saying no, either because the editorial board felt pipe smokers were not idiots and would not think of buying such a book, or that there weren't enough of them—regardless their intellect—to buy at least 5,000 copies. I think it's more the latter than the former.

Interlude ... e-books

Since writing the first edition of *Confessions*, much has changed in the realm of traditional book publishing. The business of publishing books works something like this: (1) man writes book; (2) man finds literary agent who flogs book to publishing houses; (3) author is contracted (he may receive a cash advance against royalties on sales of the book); and, (4) book is edited and marketed. The great challenge for the first-time author is many fold, but it begins with attracting an agent and then for the agent to do likewise with a publishing house. Perhaps better than 99 out of 100 authors never find an interested agent, and fewer still that land a book deal. Historically, it all reduces to economics: there's simply been no capacity or market for much of what's written, some of it quite good, most not—an author does not a writer make!—at least one worthy of a publisher's time and marketing budget. Publishers, and the agents they do business with, have always been the gatekeepers to the world of the printed book. They have the talent and experience to know what has literary merit and will make a profit, and, in general, that is their greatest motivator; and thus, the raison d'être for the vanity press, for those authors with little to nothing at stake on their writing endeavors. The only barrier to vanity and print-on-demand or POD books being the availability of money to have their work published and marketed. Enter the semiconductor.

In recent years, the business of e-commerce has spawned digital books and is in the process of rewriting the rules for how a book becomes published ... and read. A digital book is not a book in the traditional sense with two solid covers with pages between them, but a synthetic version, if you will, that is read through an electronic device with a screen. First you could only read an e-book online. Now, any one of a number of portable digital tablets, including Amazon's Kindle, Apple's iPad, Barnes and Noble's Nook, and Sony's Reader, are available to download a book to, detaching the reader from his desk- or laptop for the ultimate portable digital-reading experience, just like the traditional paper book has afforded us in mobility.

Kindle, Amazon.com's e-book reader.

The advantages to these devices are extraordinary and affect equally the writer, the publisher, and the reader. Simplistically, for the e-publisher, there's no printing just uploading from a writer, somewhere. For the author, he still has the choice of using an agent and publisher or going it alone—every author can have seemingly equal billing with established, best-selling authors, regardless of the drivel he's written. And for the reader, a book can be downloaded at a fraction of the hardcopy price (if it's even available), and an entire personal library be stored on his little book-reading tablet for reading anywhere. Can it get any better than that? Yes.

Already appearing on the horizon are applications, or "Apps," that will incorporate animations and sounds to an otherwise and classically static medium, the page. The picture of a man smoking a pipe could be made to have smoke rising from his pipe. And perhaps, if your volume is turned up, the sound of that annoying gurgle could be heard. Why leave anything to the reader's imagination? (But isn't that supposed to be one of the pleasures derived from reading a book, digital or printed?!)

Whether or not these devices will do away with the printed word of the book, magazine, and newspaper, is too soon to tell. If the survival of brick and mortar retail stores from the phenomenon of wide-spread cable TV broadband adoption from 2000–2007 is any indication, paper books and the neighborhood stores that sell them will not go the way of the dinosaur and dodo bird too quickly or completely. At least for now, the traditional book publishing business is being upset with a new rule book being written daily ... digitally.

What does any of this have to do with you, the pipeman? The pipeman reads, and for those who adopt these new reading gadgets, they will begin to find a growing number of titles on pipes and the smoking and collecting of them— both new and out-of-print titles, including works of fiction with a pipe-smoking theme, from which to purchase and download from the comfort of, well, anyplace they want to where they have a broadband connection, including wi-fi. Now, writers who perhaps didn't have the talent, time, or stamina to penetrate the traditional world of publishing or the interest to market their own print-on-demand or self-published vanity press, have the opportunity to get their manuscript—hopefully well-edited—out there for the world to consume. This could mean a rush of new smoking-related titles to market, and it will certainly give pause to the many aspiring pipemen I've corresponded with over the years about their interest to author a book on some aspect of the hobby or lifestyle. Still, the challenge for many of these pipemen, and something the semiconductor cannot magically synthesize, are the time-tested human skills needed to conceive, research, write, and edit a book. For those books that are made available for downloading, the digitally-attuned pipeman will now be able to sit in the comfort of his favorite reading chair with "book" and pipe. How traditional is that?

Back to reading and the lifestyle

It is true that people associate the pipeman with their long departed pipe-smoking uncle or grandfather. Cigars have always been equated with success. The pipe has and will always be equated with kindness and sagacity, exceptional qualities, to be sure, but hardly fashionable, sexy, or considered the *successful* image. Interestingly, those few remaining concerns with some shekels to invest in advertising might do better by advertising in magazines that do cater to pipemen of complementary pursuits and of much larger subscriber audiences. *Field & Stream*? Definitely *Cigar Aficionado*.

So what to do? Well, the magazine is what it is, so I guess you'll have to sign on for a subscription to *Esquire* to round out your education on what's needed to become a fashionable, or at least a comfortable-in-your-own-skin pipeman.

But *Esquire* could just as easily be *Fly Fisherman*, the *Atlantic* or *Playboy*. Yes, especially *Playboy*. Without doubt, in the 50 years it's been plying great four-color "articles," it has secured its position as the greatest men's lifestyle magazine ever. Tasteful, with a surprisingly broad focus, Hugh "Hef" Hefner's creation has stood the test of time and should be used as a model for other magazines, with or without the parade of air-brushed skin and manicured beavers. The point is to read, because an educated pipeman today is, well, an unexpected and cherished discovery by those he encounters.

But subscribe to *Pipes & Tobaccos* you shall and, just like the *Pipe Collector*, for as long as you can stand it. (Visit *P&T* online at www.pt-magazine.com; write to them at 5805 Faringdon Place, Suite 200, Raleigh, NC 27609.)

5

Lessons on Etiquette

Nothing is less important than which fork you use. Etiquette is the science of living. It embraces everything. It is ethics. It is honor.

—Emily Post

FEEL free to act as slovenly as you wish when alone in the confines of your home, but conduct yourself as freely in public and you'll find yourself an unwelcome guest. As a pipeman, you have the rarified charge of conducting yourself in a manner now almost relegated to the past. Knowing what to do and when to do it is something all little boys were taught, but it seems that in modern-day casual society many of the polite ways a man should interact have been superseded. You would gather that the rules of smoking a pipe would be a logical and natural extension of the basic rules of etiquette, like standing when a lady enters the room, but as practiced by far too many I know, this is clearly not the case. Given the disdain a smoker is berated with, now more than ever a conscious approach to what one does around others is not only a good idea, but also a healthy one to boot. Nevertheless, I find that even a feeble but well meaning attempt at showing a concern for another's interest and well being will usually invoke if not sympathy then an understanding and a commensurate accommodation for the smoker's passion, or as the bystander sees it, a vice.

You may not give a rat's ass for what people think of you or your behavior, but consider this: the manner in which you comport yourself, and to who may find the billowing smoke sensually odious (smoking is a selfish pursuit, n'est-ce pas?), sets a distinguishing mark you unknowingly cast upon all other pipe smokers. So, be one of the good guys and set the mark high. Set a standard for yourself that others will emulate. There's nothing to it that a little introspection and the following rules cannot remedy and keep you in high esteem in your milieu.

The pipeman's rules for public smoking

1. "Pipe-smokers are necessarily more involved with the ritual of smoking than are cigarette-smokers. After all, the pipe-smoker has many more functions to perform: He has to fill his pipe, clean it, tap it, stoke it, and keep it lit. In the process he can use it as a scratcher, pointer, drumstick, etc., which permits the use of the pipe (to stall for thinking time) as a secret signal instrument" (Gerard Nierenberg and Henry H. Calero, *How to Read a Person Like a Book*, 1990, 64). Smoking is a personal matter; keep it that way. Show reserve in your mannerisms.

2. If it is unclear as to whether or not smoking is permitted within a building, assume it's not.

3. At outdoor functions, query the host on his preference for pipe smoke around the guests.

4. Unless you're at the club, a special pipe smoker's banquet, or a meal with friends who adore the smell of your mixture, never ask for an ashtray to be brought to the table or consider exposing your pipe and smoker's paraphernalia—even when the dinner is completed.

5. Once you've studied the landscape—in or out—and are certain you have a green light, keep a vigil for reactions to both the sight of your pipe and the smoke. At first sign of trouble say not a word other than a brief apology to the offended and pocket your briar.

6. The old-fashioned strike anywhere or kitchen match is not your license to strike where you please with impunity. The match head is abrasive and will scratch even hard surfaces, even that of automobile glass. A small swipe is all that's needed to get it lit, not a long drag across the wall.

7. Smoke carries with a breeze. Do your utmost to keep downwind so that no one may be affected—even those you utterly dislike—save the gnats.

8. If your outdoor scene suddenly becomes crowded, consider pocketing your pipe or at least reducing your rate of puffing until you establish some distance.

9. Be mindful where you blow your smoke. Even a friendly pipeman will appreciate not having smoke blown full-bore in his direction.

10. When speaking, remove pipe from mouth; it is no different than what you ought not to do with food, both of which are uncouth.

    The smoking jacket and cap of Victorian times were more a practical suit (to keep the smoke off) than one of fashion, though handsome and stylish they were. Regardless, the superior ventilation of your smoking den, men's club or cigar bar, or even if you were outside taking a stroll, the wretched odor of spent tobacco has attached itself. Remove your outer garments upon re-entry, and consider a good scrubbing, especially before retiring to the boudoir replete with your wife's fineries. The potpourri can only do so much.

11. Don't smoke in a hay barn!
12. Don't smoke in someone's car unless the other passengers encourage you to do so, and then crack a window to draw out the smoke.

13. While some might find the use of a finger a quaint and practical way to tamp the top layer of ash in your pipe, don't do it; it's gauche and will brand more than your image.

14. With a jolt to your position, or reduced atmospheric pressure, hot ash and embers will fly and burn. Cease and desist upon first occasion.

15. Discard all clothing with smoke holes. Failing to do so will mark you as slapdash.

16. With time, your favorite pipe may take on a well-worn look. You make decisions about your grooming and suit of clothes for your public appearance. Why not extend this to the state of repair regarding your pipe and pouch?

17. At times, particularly for the pipeman in training, smoking activates the saliva glands. Unless you're in the woods, never spit. The embarrassment of being seen expectorating should be enough to deter even the most garish without the risk of invoking a municipal ordinance (which most do have on the books from the days when tuberculosis was the scourge). Drink a glass of water.

18. Cleaning your pipe is of interest to you alone. Retire to a safe, hidden distance to do your pipe-keeping.

19. Litter not! Dispose of pipe cleaners in a secretive way. This goes for matches, pipe cleaners and dottle. A swell trick I learned from an 'ol English pipeman was to return a spent wooden match back into its box instead of tossing it on the ground. Damp pipe cleaners should be folded and placed in a seldom-used pocket until a rubbish bin is located. (Cigarette smokers who discard their butts on the ground should be rapped on the head with the underside of a large briar. This piece of advice is less good etiquette than keeping "green," which, I think, should take preference.)

20. When there are guests, have your ashtrays cleaned regularly. And be sure to offer them your choicest tobacco and pipes to smoke.

21. Travel with a certain modicum of reserve as it relates to your tobacco and smoking possessions. Nothing so grates as the enthusiast who comes prepared with plastic tubs of everything he can manage to cram into them. How many pipes and tobaccos can one man smoke in a visit? The classic pipeman carried a pipe and a pouch. No more was needed then and this should not have changed. If you can't figure which pipe and tobacco are your current favorites, then spare everyone your indecisive wit. Pipe-bags—or man-bags as they are often called derisively—are certainly a step in the right direction, but I still believe they are unnecessary except if one is, say, traveling to an event where he wishes to boast a part of his fine collection. There is no reason why a single pipe cannot provide several consecutive smokes throughout the day if one knows what he is doing and has accomplished the no small feat of smoking dry.

22. When among fellow pipemen, it is not unusual for a chap to take a fancy to your pipe. It could be the latest in social pick-up lines, or he may have a bona fide interest in the maker's work and desire closer scrutiny. It's up to you to give it up for inspection. If you're the one asking, don't attempt this with a stranger (unless, of course, *it is* for purposes of introduction); and when the pipe is in hand, be considerate and tactful. You may consider asking this of the stranger when his pipe has gone out. Nevertheless, when a pipeman asks to see your pipe, do your best to accommodate him under the circumstances that it's probably smoldering and wet with saliva at the bit.

    Permit me to tell an amusing story. Recently, I was visiting with Richard Dunhill in his hotel suite when he asked to see the patent-era shell Canadian I was smoking. Needless to say, it was a Dunhill, in fact, one from 1939 with a deep, craggy finish upon the surface of the Algerian briar. As Richard turned it over to study its surface, a heaping of ash tumbled out onto his trouser leg. Oh dear. It was quickly brushed off. Then he proceeded to scrutinize the opposite side. Even more ash tumbled from the bowl and onto his leg. I diffused what could have been an embarrassing moment by saying it was a trick pipe. We had a good laugh and continued drinking our before-dinner Scotch.

23. Don't use your pipe as a pointer. If the pipe is lit, ash will tumble out. And there are very few who think a pipe, any pipe, is as aesthetically beautiful a thing as you consider it to be. Outside town or in the hinterlands, the pipe is as fine a tool as any for such navigational uses.

24. A man who gesticulates about wildly, arms flailing, pipe in hand, is a danger in more ways than one and should be avoided.

25. A corollary to 25 is the careless pipeman who knocks out his half-smoked pipe on an ashtray, making him an attraction and marking him a fool. First and foremost, there is nothing wasteful or imprudent with dumping a bad "bowl." As is the case with the subjective near end of a cigar, there is no disgrace in leaving the last quarter to third bowl to go to the ashtray or wind, as it is usually charged and rank with so much burning tobacco that came before it. Building a cake at the depth of a bowl is difficult, unglamorous, and not a particularly useful thing to do anyway.

26. Local smoking regulations must be obeyed regardless of their purported ridiculousness.

27. A pipe smoker in need is a sad display, and a venturesome one is always fun to be around. In both instances, be the first to extend a stranger's munificence by offering your pouch of tobacco for the chap to fill his bowl.

28. Enjoy your pipe to the fullest and in moderation—whatever that means to you—keeping in mind that smoke yellows teeth, and yellow teeth don't

sell. Consider a daily regime of oral hygiene, and every so often teeth whitening should be a consideration.

29. Be tactful in discourse with a tobacco- or pipe-maker. Let him decide what, if anything, he wishes to disclose of his process or materials. He will know much more about his trade than you ever will as a fascinated consumer. Being inquisitive also means listening more than you may be able to bear. "I like to listen. I have learned a great deal from listening carefully. Most people never listen," said Ernest Hemingway.

30. No one will care more for your preference in pipes and tobacco than you. Modesty is the rule when discussing your smokeables with others. Always do your level best to find some redeeming quality in another's stuff. Conversely, when the moment is fitting, bosom-buddies who are able to give it as good as they can take it, merit the right to hear your torturous judgment, jocularly or critically.

31. A smile or discreet wave of the hand is good form when acknowledging another pipeman's presence. There ain't many of us left, and such small gestures of support should be the unspoken word in the brotherhood.

Smoking has always demanded more of the gentleman; more so today. Most of these rules are an extension of common courtesy. When in doubt, ask for permission. When in trouble, ask for forgiveness.

6

Savoir-Faire

It is not enough to fill a pipe and put it to the mouth and set fire to it, for even the country bumpkin knows as much. It is only correct to hold it with the left hand, have the right hand provided with the stopper, impress the onlookers with majestic mien, sit in the proper attitude on the chair, and finally, to take enough time for each pipe and not treat with hasty irreverence this heavenly food.

—Peter Burmann c. 1710

IT'S French, and according to Webster's *Third New International Dictionary, Unabridged*, savoir-faire is "a seemingly instinctive ability to act appropriately in a particular situation ... adroitness in social relationships." It means knowing what to do. It may appear that some people are just better at it than others, but in my view it is anything but instinctive—it is learned from day one. And you'd better have caught on by your mid-twenties or you'll find that your station in life is moribund, having missed many exciting and important stops along the way. Courtesy, etiquette and politeness are its building blocks, but there is that aspect of comporting oneself, style, if you will, that does not come as early in life, and this is more innate than everything else. But while everyone must have a style, not all are appropriate or up to the task, whatever situation presents itself.

The previous chapter offered you guidelines for keeping you out of trouble with your pipe and may even be appreciated by others, because of your interest in not running afoul of their space. I believe that whatever your style, savoir-faire has more to do with confidence than all else. Knowing is only half; acting on it makes it whole. Do you have the wherewithal to do what you know needs doing? Most do but are slow to act, and the moment is lost.

Look, how the classic pipeman behaved in days gone by is ancient history as far as I'm concerned, though savoir-faire is never out of fashion. There is that romantic notion I struggle with that times were more genteel and nobler back 50 to 100 years, but what matters to us here and now is what you can do to elevate yourself to your own image of how you see yourself as a pipeman. Each of us has secretly wished we could be or act like someone else. That's a bad idea. Instead, use what God gave you and work at improving it. What does this have to do with smoking a pipe you ask?

Well, nothing, I guess. If you wish to learn about smoking a pipe well and other aspects of becoming a pipeman then move on to the next chapter. But something will be missing, though few will recognize this. I want you to become a pipeman in the richest sense of the term, and to do it, I need you to reflect deeply within your mantra to determine who you are, who you'd like to be and, incidentally, how a pipe can complement your stride through life. "Smoking is not only a sign of manliness, and a social habit, but it sets off a man, in certain surroundings, almost as well as a good hat or a well-tied tie. But here, as in everything else, *noblesse oblige*, and a refined man of fashion [or otherwise] must not only be careful what he smokes but how and where he indulges in the habit" (Expert Wrinkler, "Hints on Smoking," *Punch*, [London: Vol. CXXVI January–June 1904, March 9], 178). Not much has changed in 100 years of smoking when it comes to knowing the tacit rules as the "Expert Wrinkler" continues with a note on "The Dangers of Pipe-Smoking":

> Much greater latitude prevails in regard to smoking in the streets than when I was a boy, but the line must still be drawn at pipes. A cigarette or even a cigar is permissible in Bond Street, but a pipe—never. My friend, Baron Zeltinger, a very good fellow, but strangely absent-minded at times, was pilled at the National Library Club for no other reason that I could ever find out than that he had been seen smoking a meerschaum in Pall Mall. The disappointment quite broke him up, and he shortly afterwards married the daughter of a bath-chair proprietor, became a vegetarian, and now goes about in hygienic homespun. I merely mention this to show what disasters may happen to a man if he does not regulate tastes in accordance with the requirements of good form. A pipe is all very well for the privacy of the home, but for smoking in public the cigar or gold-tipped cigarette is *de rigueur*.

That was then. Still, those unspoken rules exist today, modernized, of course, but pernicious all the same. Perchance the modern-day pipeman knows this, too, and is the explanation, in part, for why one rarely sees him in public: he's self-conscious, reluctant to be singled-out, not for his incorrect choice in smoking utensils, but because the pipe—any pipe—is a relic to a time most feel we should never look back to, let alone adopt as a lifestyle. The man with his pipe, while accommodating, must carry on in the face of such adversity, all the while cutting a dashing figure.

Savoir-faire encompasses everything, following you through life like a guiding hand, presenting those silent opportunities for you to perform commendably. Certainly, it's beyond this book to enumerate those opportunities, but there is space to discuss your attitude towards those opportunities. For example, a lady walks into the office to meet you for the first time. Do you ask yourself: "Should I bother getting up, or just tell her to take a seat?" I hope the answer here is obvious. But what about when there are three other men in the office when that same guest arrives and no one rises? Then what? What do you ask yourself? "Should I let someone else initiate, or go it alone?" you wonder; "it would be the safest and least embarrassing, right?" Well, like most everything else in life, to be first is to be a winner. What about offering yourself up to embarrassment or failure in front of your peers? The successful person goes through life seizing the moment to do the right or gainful thing. He has confidence and yet is not fazed by the prospect of failure.

And with the pipe ...

Be that person of persons, perhaps with pipe firmly clenched at the moment. It is your moment to stand above the crowd to show the world that a pipe is sometimes more than just a pipe. The pipe won't always be around your every activity, to be sure, but people won't ever forget its presence, its strangeness and, if they're so opportune, the smell of its burning latakia.

Here, then, is a primer on things to consider as you move about the opportunities of life with your pipe:
1. If you're going to smoke your pipe, clench it firmly in your mouth. Holding it constantly by the shank or bowl gives you an affected style and is effeminate.
2. When leaving your den, pack only enough tobacco in your pouch to last the outing. A bulky wad in your pocket will distort the lines of your jacket. Leave all forms of manufacturer's wrappings at home.
3. It matters not how you ignite your pipe, lighter or wooden match, but never use a paper match. The lighting of your pipe is a joyous moment for the pipeman. But don't overdo the affair by blowing the flame to huge proportions or by waving your match all about the atmosphere to extinguish it; a small breath from pursed lips will suffice.
4. Carrying your pipe in any jacket pocket is risky business because of breakage, especially when you fold your arms over your chest where it so happens your pipe is located—snap! I've broken a few this way, but I feel this is still the best place to pocket your unlit pipe, upright in your outside upper or pocket-square pocket with just the tip of your pipe's mouthpiece exposed. Just be mindful. As well, if you pop into a shop for a quick purchase, place a lit pipe horizontal or nearly so in one of the lower patch pockets and let it smolder away. On leaving the shop, the pipe may still be burning, if you're lucky. Occasionally, the pipe is a real burner, and in order not to foul up the shop, you should find a small hidden place outside to set it down.

5. Too often we're rushed into making a hasty comment or decision. People are impatient by nature, and it requires a strong constitution to stave off a response, which you may not have had the requisite time to give thought to. If your pipe is handy, dig it out and study it intently; consider its construction, grain, and smoking qualities. Perchance you can divert the conversation of the interlocutor in a harmless way as you gain composure and freshen your perspective. Your answer will develop suddenly.

The British Character. Adaptability to Foreign Conditions.

6. Be as adroit with the cigar as you are with the pipe. This is not multi-tasking but good hedging.
7. Today, people stare at the pipe smoker. Adults will do so for various reasons, teenagers because they hope you're smoking pot, and children because they've probably never seen a gentleman smoking a pipe. Unless they approach you for the purpose of inquisitive conversation, ignore them. This broaches the subject of some fellows, particularly novices, who are timid about their habit. It's a perfectly natural fear and with time should fade. Believe me when I tell you that people want what you have, savoir-faire!
8. Maintain your smoking budget in a responsible way.
9. Realize that a pipe is a means to an end—to smoke tobacco; to appreciate that, more often than not, love of an individual briar is fleeting.

10. Try and develop an understanding and a critical eye for good, established design that is well executed.

11. The pipeman is patient. He can look at 1000 pipes before he finds the one that is just right. This not being picky. This is being discriminate. Just do it with resolute and swift action. A far more complicated endeavor than tasting different porridges for the one at just the right temperature, I can assure you.

With or without the pipe, see yourself as a man of can-do-right spirit. And no one will ever know about the mystical quality of savoir-faire that the pipe has bestowed on you.

7

Dunhill is Dead. Long Live Dunhill

Death is a very dull, dreary affair, and my advice to you is to have nothing whatsoever to do with it.

—W. Somerset Maugham

THERE are some who will beat a dead horse. They will strike and return yet again to extract their pound of flesh, but all for naught, for that which once was has long since departed. As recently as the autumn of '08, I was a member in good standing with the Pipe Club of London, but that all changed with an editorial comment in their semi-annual newsletter, the *Journal*, a compact, 40-page, B&W affair. It got me thinking about whether the investment of membership renewal—a no small sum of $50—was money I could use better elsewhere. The comment was by the club's latest installment of a secretary and treasurer, Michael P. Gratrick, and was an odious reference to Dunhills as "Dunghills" (issue 29, p. 18). I thought the reference to be in rather poor taste, so I wrote to Mr. Gratrick, objected to the unflattering remark, and demanded a retraction. As far as I could recall in my eight years as a member, the Dunhill Company had always acted kindly to the PCoL, supporting it in any way it could, including hosting its slow-smoke competition, the Radford Cup, at its Duke Street shop. I was ill at ease of being associated with a reputable organization that slandered the good name of such an historical stalwart of the pipe and tobacco trade. Indeed, there is no other firm which is endeared by so many and with such reverential affection as "Dunhills." Gratrick thought otherwise and was clearly intent on a further whipping of the Dunhill horse in his email reply to me December of the same year: "Dunghill is as far as I (and a lot of others here) am concerned, are an over-priced supermarket, a mere travesty of the company that forged such a fine history, which has been discarded through corporate greed. Though they are, we note, willing to trade on the name made so famous in that history."

I was dissatisfied with the remark and, hoping for clearer thinking, returned to my desktop for another email to the club's long-standing member, former secretary and treasurer, now Life President, and friend, Peter C. Wiseman. It was not to be had. PCW had this to say: "We are beset from all corners by the 'anti-smoking' establishment, and do not wish to hide behind a screen of timidity, but must respond, even in jest, to apparent failures in the pipe and tobacco world as we see them. [Dunhill a "failure"? We shall see.] It is true that the sense of humour in the U.K. is not always compatible with that of the U.S.A., and is sometimes misunderstood."

Was I wrong? Did I miss the humor—the British humor—in such a belittlement? Was *I* now beating this issue as one would a dead horse? I did not think so. More importantly, why introduce this chapter with such a cheap and pathetic journalistic barb as this to the apparent demise of the finest briar and tobacco enterprise in the history of Smokedom?

But wait. Issue 29 of the *Journal* offered more! This time, a reprint of a letter addressed to the Dunhill company from an anonymous and, as we'll see, misguided American PCoL member, pleading with the Dunhill firm to re-examine their recent decision to curtail U.S. exports of their standard tinned mixtures, like Elizabethan, Durbar, and London Mixture. I was puzzled why the contributor deemed it necessary to conceal his identity for his letter was sincere and polite in tone. At any rate, the nameless pipeman was clearly frustrated with his plight because, according to him, American blends don't stack up to even the EU-fabricated Dunhill mixtures, and he considers "blotting out the white dots or turn the stem upside down so the dot can't be noticed"; and "that he'll "think twice before purchasing another Dunhill pipe!" (The Dunhill trademark is correctly referred to as the white spot, not dot.) I pity the fellow as he clearly has a dilemma. Had he known of the ban in advance, I suspect he would have taken in as much stock as he felt he could handle for cellaring. And are Dunhill white spot pipes at all related to Dunhill-brand tobacco?

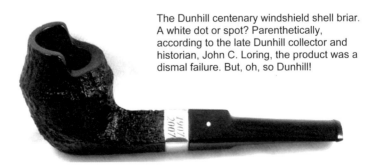

The Dunhill centenary windshield shell briar. A white dot or spot? Parenthetically, according to the late Dunhill collector and historian, John C. Loring, the product was a dismal failure. But, oh, so Dunhill!

These three voices rising from the printed and electronic page of such a well-respected club (with an international membership numbering roughly 350) is telling and symbolic of a sentiment I myself have broached in my brooding over the state of affairs of Anglo-loyal pipe smokers, and I know there are others as well that have pondered what will be, but chiefly in regards to Dunhill. Why pick on Dunhill? Surely there are other pipe and tobacco firms which one could wax disappointment and disdain upon. Those firms that cling with one remaining finger to a trade that is now all but gone. In point of fact, Dunhill is an excellent example to further this story. You see, Dunhill survived! More than that, they grew; they evolved, and today, almost everyone in the civilized world of at least a moderate income and sense of the finer manly accoutrements, recognizes the name and its distinctive mark (and I'm not talking about the white spot). The same cannot be said of any other enterprise in the realm in which pipe smokers dwell.

Not very long ago, I asked Richard Dunhill, son of Vernon Dunhill, and grandson to and patriarch of every pipeman of distinction, Alfred Dunhill, how much longer the firm would continue applying their old white spot mark to briar pipes and other fancy smoking items. Although long since retired, he replied jocularly, "until they're down to making just one pipe." Cold comfort, to be sure, and if certain market trends continue, this moment may be closer than anyone hopes. The loss would be great, or would it? Old traditions die hard but only if there's anyone left to notice.

Now for a bit of corporate hopscotch.

Dunhill ceased producing tobacco in 1981 when they sold the division, Dunhill Tobacco Ltd., to Rothmans International PLC, who at that time had an ownership interest in Alfred Dunhill Ltd. Rothmans moved the brand to Belfast where they were already having their other pipe blends done up by Murray Sons & Co. Ltd., a Rothman's company. Fast forward to present. The current owner of Dunhill Tobacco Ltd. is the tobacco conglomerate BAT, British-American Tobacco. The point is, '81 was the year when the Dunhill you and I know for its white spot pipes and My Mixture tobaccos, completely divested itself from ownership, manufacture, and marketing of Dunhill tobaccos. The move, I'm told by a company insider at the time, was because pressure was brought to bear by the anti-tobacco establishment (including government) to not have tobacco revenues finance other "legitimate" non-tobacco operations. And recently, as previously noted elsewhere in this book, production moved from Ireland to Denmark, where Orlik now does it up. Nonetheless, Dunhill does still produce pipes along with men's haberdashery items, including leather goods, lighters, pens, Italian wool suits, and watches under the ownership of Switzerland-based, luxury-goods conglomerate,

Richemont Group. And get this, Richemont holds a significant ownership in BAT! I don't know about you, but my head is spinning from all of this corporate hopscotching.

So does the Dunhill tobacco of today have anything to do with the Dunhill tobacco of pre-1981, when it was family owned? In terms of ownership, as we have seen, absolutely nothing. In terms of branded product, it is what it is, Dunhill-brand tobacco. Nevertheless, I've heard from pipemen from many corners of the pipe-smoking world who claim the mixture recipes have changed as production has moved from Dunhill to Murray to Orlik.

I can appreciate the long-running debate among pipemen as to how the original London-made Dunhill tobacco was superior to everything that came afterwards. Whatever your thoughts are on this evolutionary matter, I find I'm unable and unwilling to blame the Dunhills (Richard, specifically, as the last family member working in the business) for getting out of the tobacco business like they did. Keeping in mind that tobacco blending was, I believe, the third business Alfred Dunhill got into. Even still, I'll hazard to bet that the economics of the decision to divest beat the nostalgia of commercial tradition hands down.

So, are you, like the anonymous PCoL chap who wrote to Dunhill to complain, upset that those famous My Mixture tinned tobaccos are no longer available at your favorite tobacconist or e-tailer? If yes, fine, but do not blame Dunhill, or its owner, Richemont Group. It is not their product! Certainly do not dishonor them as the PCoL has by mocking them with a juvenile-like bastardizing of the name. Write and grumble to BAT.

What about white spot briars? Strictly speaking, briar pipes were not tobacco, and Dunhill/Richemont did hang on to that business. Here, the debate has raged on two fronts: out-of-country ebauchon turning, and the demise of oil curing.

I visited two Dunhill pipe factories in 2001. I did not observe any bowls being turned or fraized, nor did I see any pipes being oil-cured. I did not ask the reason why that was for I knew the answers even then. Why should it matter where Dunhill chooses to manufacture all or a portion of its famous 90 steps of production? Clearly, the firm wishes to turn a profit and so—like many others we know of and those still to be discovered—moved offshore to Spain for ebauchon turning. The pipes are still legally marked "Made in England," and that should be enough, and I believe it is to many who choose not to delve into the finer aspects of a manufactured product such as their smokeables. But clearly, the pipe fanatics of the hobby object at the loss and lament for the days of old—if they were ever around then—for the 100 percent London production at Walthamstow, or earlier, in Plaistow.

I understand this. I mean, who goes out of their way—and at such expense—to purchase the finest British pipe, knowing full well that half of the pipe had been fabricated in Spain! It used to trouble me, but only somewhat, because when I come across a smashing new Dunhill pipe, it matters not one iota that the piece is not 100 percent British. Look, the briar root is Mediterranean, and the vulcanite is German. So what are you supposed to call the thing? It's really no different than an automobile or an airplane, where for so long, outsourcing to foreign lands has been the standard practice. Where it all comes together, at assembly, is the pipe's country of origin and why it should be stamped so. I think what is key to the consumer is that the same exacting high standards of craftsmanship still reign supreme with Dunhill goods, whether its pipes are partially made in Spain or, for instance, its leather goods, are stitched up in Germany.

As to oil-curing, something that, like sandblasting, Dunhill invented, what are we to make of statements from those knowledgeable of the trade and Dunhill, who claim the firm did away with the oil process at least since the early 1960s? Oil curing was part of the original sandblasting process on Shell models. Did it also affect taste? That nut-like taste people refer to? Did it contribute to the wood being more fire retardant? All subjective stuff really. It's all just typical fun and harmless banter that every hobby spins on.

I'm amused by the pipe weenies and the blogs they prattle on. They are convinced that because they have been around a few years smoking Dunhills, that what they profess to know is the way it is. And to those that are despondent on recent briar production quality or critical of a firm they know little about, shame on them for their cheap talk. Don't be the one swayed into entering into such frivolous discussions. Be that pipeman with good rational balance for knowing what matters and what does not. Let us put things into further, lucid perspective.

Where are all the original English pipe firms of recent memory? From BBB to Loewé to Sasieni, they're either dead or part of a pipe-brand conglomerate where all of the brands are made under the same factory roof by one or more craftsmen. Their former distinction is gone. But not Dunhill. Not because they necessarily made a better pipe than, say, Charatan—their artistic arch rival for so many years—but because they were better businessmen. They diversified long before it was chic to be anti-smoking, because it was prudent for pipes to be a means to an end, not the be-all-end-all. Today, Alfred Dunhill Ltd. contributes about €309M revenue to the coffers of its owner, publicly-traded Richemont Group (no clues are given to the contribution made by its "smokeables"). Paging through the firm's 2007 annual report, you'll see no mention of pipes. In fact, the Dunhill business is referred to as Leather Goods! A digital word search through the annual report makes any mention of pipe goods or the white spot. Surprised? Don't be. And I wasn't surprised to read that one of the biggest things going for the business is the installment of barbershops in the stores that have the room, because I saw it at their London shop. When I was there in the spring of 2008, I also noticed a few small glass cases of briars tucked away in a dark corner, but I could tell the female clerk wasn't at all interested in discussing the finer points of this merchandise, and would have much preferred talking up their very fine £1,850 wool suits. Earlier in the decade when I visited the shop, the entire mezzanine level, which was one-half humidor room and lounge, one-half pipe shop, had now been "updated" to exclude any shred of tobacco and briar, replaced with an old-fashioned barber chair and more fashion.

If you are new to the pipe-smoking lifestyle and visit a Dunhill shop, anywhere, you would be hard pressed to see what if anything Alfred Dunhill ever had to do with smoking. What's more, if they had not already distanced themselves enough from any lingering scent of tobacco, last year Richemont spun off their 30 percent stake in BAT to a separate company—much like Dunhill did with its tobacco almost 30 years ago now. For the life of me, I cannot fathom why Dunhill remains in the pipe business altogether.

Today, Dunhill stands for the finest in men's clothing and other furnishings, with the international face of Dunhill being the British actor Jude Law. Had Dunhill promoted such a heartthrob 50 years ago he would have most certainly smoked a pipe. Today, one could easily imagine Mr. Law's Dunhill contract specifically forbidding him from smoking!

So, after all that has been said and done by the naysayers to Dunhill's evolution, are we to castigate Dunhill for their apparent failures? Look, they bowed to the anti-smoking lobby, didn't they? I mean, their mixtures are no longer theirs. (How on earth can we be sure of what those crafty, sugar-lovin' Danes are now subjecting our favorite English mixtures to?) And shame on them for changing their pipe manufacturing process we admired so much. For all it is worth, it is a pity they divulged these things to begin with, because it never really mattered. Dunhill may be an old firm, now well into its second century of continuous operations, but they remain young and fresh with new ideas and innovations—incredibly, even with their old-line briar pipes! I imagine company founder, Alfred Dunhill, who almost chose the road of candy production over that of tobacco and pipes, would be tickled things have worked out so well. And I think it's a fitting tribute to him that current management are reluctant to give up that mark of excellence from whence it all began, the white spot.

8

Cigars by Far

The moment of choosing a cigar is an important, difficult, and decisive one. Whether you are in the home of friends or in a cigar store stocking the latest Havana cigars, your decision should be weighed intelligently and according to the situation in which you find yourself. Never should the choice be an offhand matter. A cigar ought always to be an event.

—Zino Davidoff, *The Connoisseur's Book of the Cigar*

CIGARS are different. You may not be a cigarman yet, but if you appreciate the pipe chances are you'll understand what the sexy fuss over cigars is, and you'd better know what to do with one when offered to accompany someone in a smoke, or your future at the firm or clique may be in jeopardy.

As simple as the cigar may seem to be—no moving parts, right?—the seasoned stogie-man will be only too glad to talk your ear off about the choices, complexities and contentment that the cigar bestows. But like the pipe, Grasshopper, you must first learn its ways. That, in itself, is a book. And just such a book exists, which saves me the task of having to explain it all to you. Zino Davidoff—my great-uncle on my mother's side—wrote such a book in 1967, and to this day it remains the cigar aficionado's bible for the savoir-faire of cigar-smoking. The *Connoisseur's Book of the Cigar* is on the reading list noted in chapter 4. There's nothing I would consider adding to such a masterpiece without risk of embarrassing myself.

You say, I'm a pipeman. I don't need to know about cigars, so why unload a Hamilton or Jackson on such a used book? A short story will help explain what I mean.

Let's say you've been invited to spend the afternoon at the country residence of Richard Dunhill. Ah, Dunhill, the icon of British pipe mastery for 100 years. You figure on taking your best Dunhill with you if the occasion presents itself for a smoke. It does! You and Richard are enjoying the afternoon sun in his solarium with a Scotch, when he insists it's time to smoke. You remove your pipe from your pocket and smoke it. Later, Richard asks to

see your pipe, and boy, are you glad it's not a Continental job but a White Spot
Dunhill. Afterwards, lunch is served by Richard's wife, Pat, and it's delightful.
At coffee, Richard steals away shortly re-emerging with several cigars which
he claims are the best money can buy. They're Dunhills, of course. In fact,
they're quite rare 25-year-old, long-out-of-production Havana Club Selections,
Churchills, in fact. Right. You know what they are and what to do. Now would
be a bad time to ask which end to light.

The pipeman
would be well
advised to
occasionally set
pipe aside and
appreciate the
pleasures
bestowed by
the cigar.

The situation is all too possible, though with different people and
circumstances, of course. However, the story is true, because I was that person
at Dunhill's estate ... and smoking that cigar with Richard was a breathtaking
moment. (And he was right about that cigar being the best money could buy.)

Do your utmost to be prepared for whatever smoking circumstances you
may encounter. Get the Davidoff book!

9

The Right Pipe

*No pipe ever really rivaled the briar in my affections, though I can
recall a mad month when I fell in love with two little meerschaums,
which I christened Romulus and Remus. They lay together in one
case in Regent Street, and it was with difficulty that I could pass the
shop without going in. Often I took side streets to escape their
glances, but at last I asked the price. It startled me, and I hurried
home to the briar.*

—J.M. Barrie, *My Lady Nicotine*

YOU'LL come to find that Barrie was right; that while you may
wander—or as with Barrie's fictional pipeman, become confused and
distracted—in your smoking choices from time to time, the type of
pipe made from the briar root is the one you'll come back to time and again for
the most satisfaction. There is a host of reasons for this. Oh, there are those
few poor souls who tried meerschaums and fell in love and decided to stick to
them. And some I know who secretly prefer the clay, but will never admit it to
me. There must be numerous who found true solace in smoking the calabash
exclusively, yet I know of only three. Indeed, there are those pipemen, keister
stuck to a tractor seat, who will never smoke anything but the earthy corncob. I
pity them all for they lost their way back home to the only pipe that should be
smoked regular-like.

Root briar, as it is sometimes called and so branded, is the best all-rounder
for the pipeman. It's the most consistent, dependable, durable, handsome,
omnipresent, portable, recyclable, and satisfying. One could easily continue
traversing the alphabet finding fitting appellations to describe this 150-year-
old wood-type pipe. Study history and you will find countless references and
stories concerning the briar: nothing mean-spirited has ever affixed itself to the
gnarled root wrested from the ground. The same cannot be said of all the other
pipes fashioned from different materials.

There is never a wrong time to light up a briar, inside or out; country or
city; stoked with matured Virginia or full-English flake, the briar is sovereign.
I proclaim it thus as does every pipeman worth his salt. A superior material
will never be found even in this fast-paced day of gee-whiz material

discoveries. Moore's Law will never be applied to the pipe, because I'm entirely convinced no one is searching for a material to better briar.

The pipes that don't fit in

In your wanderings you'll see them. They'll sit there apart and forlornly, relics from another time. In a shop or antique fair, at a country auction or online, you'll spy it; a pipe for sure, but not what you know. They go by many names: calabash, clay, corn cob, hookah, meerschaum, metal, porcelain, Tyrolean, Ulmer, and more. If you think the briar has one foot in the grave, then these other types have both with the earth falling in all around. But however small their numbers, devotees go quietly about collecting and smoking them. How odd. How so pipeman-like. These pipes, these anachronisms from Smokedom's past just won't go away, and you'll do well by understanding each of them so that you'll not only appreciate more what a blessing the briar is, but also because you are a pipeman and must be fairly conversant in the history of all pipes.

Meerschaum is a fine pipe material and has been much longer in use than briar. Like the calabash, it seems that if you're smitten with pipes—whatever you do with them—you need at least a few to be taken seriously by other pipemen. And what awkwardness to actually be talking to a complete stranger who, when discovering you're a pipeman, asks if you have meerschaum pipes in your repertoire when you do not. But a good knowledge of what meerschaum is will be effective subterfuge in the interim. The history of meerschaum and pipes made from this porous, lightweight material, is a fascinating story still being carried out in the shallow and dangerous mines of Eskişehir, Turkey. Pipes are typically carved into all sorts of likenesses by artisans of varying proficiency; are fitted out with a case to protect the easily damaged stone; and have the potential of changing color during its smoking, from its natural pure white to a deep golden brown.

Therein lays the problem. There's never been a surefire way to color a meerschaum pipe … well. And try as you may, the pipe is typically wayward. There are many who profess that the smoke from a meerschaum is earthy and don't like it. In a typical foreigner's view of American fashion, Turkish carvers believe us Yankees desire the colossal and garish, and so produce ungainly smoking pieces that would be difficult to pocket, freakish to be seen on the public green smoking and, so, nothing but a stay-at-home smoker or artwork to be cherished while displayed in a living-room cabinet or *étagère*.

I have found well-executed, carved meerschaum pipes to be beguiling but have resisted temptation and stayed on the side of briar. A noted collector friend urged me not to collect the finer antique specimens from the period 1850–1925, the craft's zenith because, at least to the world of pipes, this was if not the passion of monarchs then the pursuit of the wealthy. And so I admire them from afar and have read extensively about this fascinating material.

Metal, I'm sad to say, has been used in the construct of a few pipe brands. The very thought of placing metal—aluminum to be specific—next to a bowl of briar is sacrilege and turns my stomach. And what for? The manufacturers will declare that the metal shank cools and condenses the moisture-laden smoke, thereby conveying a dry smoke. True enough. But the pipeman who smokes the right tobacco in the right pipe need not be troubled with this mechanical thingamabob to get on with it. Never purchase one! Destroy any given to you as a gift, and distance yourself from those who take them, or you risk an association and your existence will be quickly forgotten by those who know.

But I would be remiss if I did not tender my impressions on the design of one brand: Kirsten of Seattle. From time to time, I find myself drawn to its streamline shape and superbly manufactured qualities. The ultimate gadget pipe (aren't pipemen also the consummate gadget geeks?), I often expect to find a tiny compass, small length of line and fishing hook contained secretly within. Nonetheless, I've yet to fall victim to its sleek allure by putting one to my lips.

Clay pipes have been around the longest and are purportedly still being produced in staggering numbers that easily rival briar, though this is rather puzzling, since these rather "earthy" pipemen are never about. Like meerschaum, the history of the clay is absorbing (pun intended) and well worth your study. I've smoked clays and have found the better ones to smoke divinely. They color quickly with a bowl-creeping, sickly looking brown tar that is, well, comforting. They're an excellent adjunct to a formal pipeman's dinner as a quaint after-dinner smoke or, as my club does it, as part of a ritualistic ceremony at its annual dinner. Smoking a clay takes you back centuries to the city and country inns of merry olde England, giving you a taste very true of the day. Needless to say, they're inexpensive, will break under the slightest heavy hand, and are becoming a challenge to locate, particularly the longer churchwarden variety.

Calabash is a gourd of South Africa and a pipe whose genesis was the time of the Boer War. I know too much of this pipe type to want to regurgitate it—again—to you, but I will say that your best smoke will come from one. (The *History of the Calabash Pipe*, that book I published in 2006, met with more enthusiasm than I had expected, and is now being prepared for a second, all-color edition.)

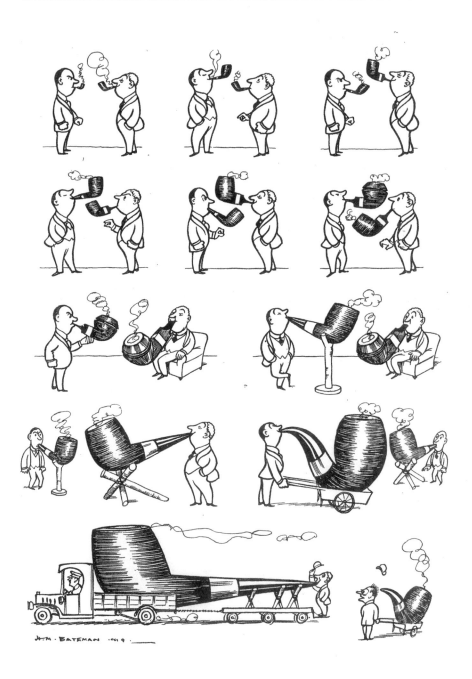

No Briar Without a Thorn.

As pipes go, it's a jewel of a smoke, but even old hands of the briar are unfamiliar with its smoking qualities because, I believe, it's a bizarre looking contraption. Yet everyone who sees it knows what it is, including non-smokers. No pipe shape better symbolizes the pipeman and tobacconist of old than the calabash because of its association with that pipe-wielding Great Detective, Sherlock Holmes—with books still in print. (And strange as it is, Holmes's creator, Sir Arthur Conan Doyle, also smoked a calabash, but he never did outfit the sleuth with anything but briars and clays, though the many novels make reference to non-descript pipes.)

But if the ultimate objective to pipe smoking is to derive maximum pleasure from the burning of tobacco, why, indeed, is the calabash no longer seen as the right pipe? It wasn't always so. From the time the 'bash was introduced in London around 1905 through the first Great War, its popularity as a novel pipe was unsurpassed, and the greatest English pipe manufactory of the time, Adolph Frankau and Company (BBB brand), flooded the market with exquisite product for many eager pipemen to savor. The fad held on with pipemen for about 10 years. The briar was never in fear of being supplanted by the calabash, and solid production and demand for it continued through the 1970s until things basically tanked. Now there is only one firm in Austria that struggles with it and I believe still finds a ready market for the few that it ships from its loading dock.

As pipes go, the calabash tends to be a relatively gigantic affair and, as has always been reported, is best left next to the wingback for a contemplative smoke as a fire crackles away in the hearth and you digest a good book and a whiskey. And I would posit, that if you're banished to the garage or back porch, the calabash is still a first-rate smoke and will deliver the truest taste of your burning tobacco—better even than a briar. A smoke better than a briar? Preposterous! Why not? Fact is, there are many well-cut briars that smoke miserably and no one really knows why. The calabash is one instrument of smoking that looks distinguished, indeed, eccentric and, most important, performs consistently superbly. This is because the large natural void afforded by the gourd tames the smoke and heat and delivers what every pipeman demands, full flavor. As a bonus, the gourd —unlike the troublesome meerschaum—colors quickly and evenly, giving you something to show for your allegiance to it. Get one or two—to be a pipeman requires it. And if you have a flair for the bold, bring one out at a special event and you'll stand out among that relentless brown sea of briars.

Corn cob pipes are only suitable for the bucolic lifestyle, farmland specifically. Don't be caught dead smoking one away from your tractor on the back forty or you'll be branded a yokel. The only positive thing I've heard stated on corn cobs is that they're cheap—a good throw-away pipe—so why bother. And don't start with General Douglas MacArthur smoked one. He smoked briars. His publicity shots were taken with oversized corn cobs because, as was said at the time, it was patriotic. Speaking of MacArthur and his "cob," for those among the brotherhood of pipemen who are nostalgic and pine for Americana, seek out the film Medal of Honor, 2000, starring Robert DeNiro and Cuba Gooding, Jr. DeNiro portrays a U.S. Navy Master Chief salvage diver who smokes a corn cob MacArthur was supposed to have given him during the war. DeNiro smoked it well and apparently for way too many years!

[Purchasing the right pipe is not always an easy decision.]

The right pipe for you

So now that I've rattled on sufficiently about those pipes not to smoke or at least to smoke only at an appropriate place and time, we come back to, you guessed it, the briar. And as the genus of briars goes, there are but two types or styles, if you will: straights and bents. Within each type there's a dizzying array of shapes from which to choose. There are the classics, and then the manufacturer's or artisan's attempt at variations. Which one is right for you? Most pipemen will say that there is no right or best shape. That to each his own is the rule to follow, many will opine. I will say that the straight pipe, the billiard and all its classic variations, like the Canadian, Dublin, Liverpool, Lovat, and pot, are it. The preponderance of pipes produced have been straights, regardless of shape. Whether you're well built or wiry, or something in between, a straight pipe will suit you admirably. Why? They just look better, smoke better, and follow in the tradition of British pipemen, a race of men to which there will never be an equal. "An extraordinary instance of the demand for our goods in the U.S.A. is the case of Dunhill pipes. The amazing vogue for these pipes in America is solely due to the fact that the American looks upon the Englishman as one who knows and appreciates a good pipe" (Stefan Schwarzkopf, "Who Said 'Americanization'?: The Case of Twentieth-Century Advertising and Mass Marketing from a British Perspective," originally published in *Advertising World*, April 1924; Jessica C.E. Gienow-Hecht, ed., *Decentering America*, [Oxford and New York: Berghahn Books, 2008], 41).

Speaking of body type, I do believe that some pipe shapes look better on the man than others. But that's for you to decide—just keep to straights. One cardinal rule: slender men should select straight shapes; while large men should select large straights. I will confess that bents do fit some men better than others. Oh, you'll dally hither and thither thinking that all shapes are fair game, and they are, but in time you'll come to the realization that straights, especially the billiard and Dublin, are unsurpassed instruments to smoking heaven.

With the first printing of this book came a reminder by more than one senior pipeman at my club that straights are all well and good but their dental work is often less than accommodating in supporting such a smoldering cantilever. It is far easier for them to smoke a bent. That much of mechanical engineering I can understand. So in the spirit of gentlemanly compromise, I will acquiesce.

Used pipes

I believe it is within every pipeman to have an affinity towards the old and historic. Whether your interest in antiquity is knowledge-based or as a collector of dusty articles, the world of pipes holds great prospect. The recommended reading list in chapter 4 includes some wonderful examples of old books that tell great stories of the way it used to be in Smokedom. If your penchant is for the material and functional, then there is no dearth of old, used briar pipes to select from. Often referred to arbitrarily as estate pipes in online markets, with the largest, eBay, these previously owned or used pipes can turn out to be the cat's meow. You'll spend less than half of what new pipes sell for; get a pipe that has been broken-in for you (no small feat); experience old-world craftsmanship, particularly from early British marks; learn a great deal about pipes and assorted smoking paraphernalia; and, perhaps best of all, enjoy a nail-biting good chase participating in the online auction game. A well-worn nugget of advice: caveat emptor. Believe none of what the seller says and only half of what is pictured. In due time you will begin to recognize reputable sellers who specialize in used briars and come to trust their listings, still oftentimes chock-full of hyperbole and supposition. (See chapter 12 for more.)

Buy American

If it were only that easy. The best pipe you can smoke, I would argue, is any British mark from the 1950s. Many can still be had at a reasonable price and in smokeable condition. America did have many pipemakers then, some of them large, like S.M. Frank with their brand Kaywoodie, but they always played second fiddle to the Brits in terms of quality and pedigree. Today, there is an emerging class of talented U.S. artisan pipesmiths whittling away in their spare time. Their wares demand your close scrutiny. Most of the stuff I've reviewed at pipe shows is first-rate in quality and, sometimes, in design, as classic shapes go. Paying more for a "home" pipe, new or used, will be your decision, but it will always be the correct one in my book.

My decision was made early on to smoke only British-made pipes from the 1950s to the 1970s, earlier still if the value is evident and the price right. Of course, as any tried pipeman worth his dottle will attest, I will not pay a sum more than $25 for such used pipes because, well, this is all that my wife believes a used pipe can cost. So why make things difficult?

10

The Right Tobacco

Perfection is such a nuisance that I often regret having cured myself of using tobacco.
— Emile Zola

UNHILL My Mixture 965 was the mixture I used to instructed new pipe smokers to start with. It was one of the finest English tobaccos ever made: it smoked dry; was of a medium strength; kept lit effortlessly; was great tasting; and was acquired at a reasonable price. Many experienced pipemen agreed with me on this point and continue to smoke this mixture with regularity without being swayed by the latest tobacco flavor, that is, the few who were prudent enough to safeguard for the eventuality when it would become unavailable. Nevertheless, with 965 no longer being made available here, pipemen have sought their alternative. Many have since switched to the Pease mark because of Greg Pease's slight of hand in creating such majestically-tasting English varieties; and this author has endorsed his acumen for blending by establishing it as the pipeman's benchmark. Yet there are those peculiar fellows who tire easily of the things that are and want the strange and new. As with food, there is a range of tobacco offerings for every taste, albeit within a much narrower spectrum. And while there are, strictly speaking, but three types of tobacco leaf to choose from—burley, flue-cured, and Oriental—there are umpteen processed tobacco mixtures. With time, the pipeman knows what works for him and what doesn't. Along this tobacco road there are many rewarding discoveries with an equal number of dismal failures to experience. I know one seasoned pipeman in my club who will smoke anything and everything and relish the puff of each selection equally. Bless him for he is one of the few.

Aromatics

These are my confessions, so I will begin this chapter by telling you that the worst tobacco concoctions ever created are those categorized as aromatics. I know this to be true, because I have led more than a few up-and-coming pipemen out of that sickly hot, sweet, and wet jungle of aromatics to that blissful place known only to the experienced pipeman as English. Market statistics, though, handily—and deceptively— prove me incorrect in this assertion, and I know why. First, the vast majority of pipe tobacco sold in this country is at the supermarket. The supermarket carries aromatics—typically a burley and Cavendish mixture smothered in artificial essences, sweetener, and a preservative with the questionably sounding food chemical ingredient, propylene glycol. (Propylene glycol, by the way, is not that green stuff you put in your radiator as an engine coolant—that's ethylene glycol; in fact, it's anything but a coolant, but does perform similarly in the pouch or humidor to extend the life of your tobacco—as a humectant—and, I contest, fouls your briar quite handily.) Second, bystanders to a "lit" pipeman rarely object to the fruity fragrance of his smoke, so different from the odor of the cigar and cigarette. Now if that pipeman were smoking an English mixture containing Orientals (in olden days, referred to as aromatics), Virginias and, typically, including latakia, the collateral comments would be markedly different. It would be that of disgust, because, you see, true English blends do not contain added artificial sweeteners, fruity flavor enhancers, or gooey glycol. English mixtures, light- to full-bodied, taste and smell wonderful to the pipeman, but he is often puzzled by the lack of enthusiasm expressed by the onlooker. So the pipeman has slowly evolved into a sort of patsy smoking his "approved" aromatics just so he could get on with his pipes in public, offending as few as possible. After a while, aromatics, like the Cavendish type, seem to be a suitable smoke for his constitution.

What a shame. If there's one thing that has spoiled the future of many a hopeful pipeman it is the well-meaning but woefully-ignorant tobacconist or, indeed, pipe smoker, pushing his aromatic tobacco. (Aromatics wouldn't be the end of the world for the beginner, but when it's coupled with a poorly packed pipe—one packed too loosely or too densely—it will be. In either scenario, the pipe smoker will be over working the combustion process and really getting his little furnace too hot for the liking of his tongue.) Incredibly, the singed-tongue syndrome is nothing new. Writing in his memoirs *Forty Years of Spy* (Great Britain: Brentano's, 1915, 294), caricaturist for the original *Vanity Fair* magazine, Leslie "Spy" Ward, recounted this tobacco-salient tale as the most famous stage actor of Sherlock Holmes sat for his drawing in 1907:

> When Mr. William Gillette sat for me in dressing gown and pipe, I did not have to request him to smile, for a serious and contemplative gaze was quite in keeping with his *rôle* of Sherlock Holmes. During our conversation he asked me if I could recommend a good tobacco, because the brand he smoked on stage burnt his tongue. I suggested "Log Cabin," and at our next meeting asked if he had acted on my recommendation, and if he found the result satisfactory; but "Log Cabin," in spite of its merits and mildness, was not suitable for dramatic service as it took too long to light.

Shocking! Holmes did not know how to smoke! We'll never know why Gillette was having trouble with his briar, but I'll bet it had something to do with the variables surrounding his little combustion process: tobacco mixture, how he packed it in the bowl, and smoking style. It's been the same sad fixture for decades. But how does the nascent pipeman know what to do when the best of tobaccos—the ones which are best for the new smoker—are hidden from view, known only, it seems, to pipemen of age and experience?

American actor William Gillette as Sherlock Holmes by Spy.
in ... *The Case of the Burnt Tongue*?

First, he should avoid any tobacco made in Denmark. If there's one country that gets on better these days with producing the bulk of the world's pipe-smoking tobacco (apparently 70 percent of it), it's Denmark. This fact has more to do with the western world's changing economic and political landscape facing smoking than that of Denmark loving its tobacco and pipemen. Nonetheless, it's not an exaggeration to state that this wee-little country must have regular national surpluses of liquid invert sugar, because what they call their English blends are clotted with the stuff. I've yet to taste better than a fair-to-middling quality English mixture from the land of Hans Christian Andersen.

The Germans, like their much larger tobacco-producing Danish neighbors, who either own or private-label many of the fine old English and Scottish mixtures, have, in my mind, done a disservice to pipemen by trying to carry on the old standards, because I don't think it can be done without change. It's not fair to the legacy of the brand, nor is it fair to the pipemen who cut their first briar-teeth on the original stuff. You might posit that it makes no difference, because the number of pipemen around now who were around in the day of the original factory production are fewer. Some care, some don't, and some have long ago moved on to greener pastures. There are some who try their best to describe how the mixture has changed, but I think this is a very difficult and subjective thing to do. And it's really quite disconcerting for the up-and-coming pipeman to keep hearing that the old-time mixture was much better when it was still produced back in the Isles.

It's like single-malt Scotch whiskey. Connoisseurs of the Highland or Islay dram know that everything contributes to the final taste, including the shape of the still, the malting, volume of peat smoke, burn water, proximity to the sea, cellaring conditions, barrel oak type, the stillman, and even certain cobwebs! It is no less for the production of a tobacco if it is to have consistency through the years. No one really expects the mixtures to be faithfully reproduced in a different country and under the nose of a different master blender. Like the Danes, I don't think the Germans have it in them to produce a good English mixture. But business is business and goodwill in the brand persists enough to still make a tidy sum from its production. As they say, business before pleasure. But for the pipeman, business don't trump pleasure when it comes to a satisfying smoke from your old favorite. You decide.

If it meant that the pipeman would be safe by excluding Danish and German tobacco he'd have an easy go of it. But tobaccomen are clever and disguise their adulterated wares to entice and fool the gullible and unwary. They do this by producing fabulously colorful pouch and tin labels that tug at the heartstrings. If you're a fisherman, they'll have a tobacco with a label just for you. If you're a dog lover, they'll have a tobacco just for you as well. And on and on. Tobaccos with names of romantic cities or countrified American slang are other useful propaganda ploys they exploit to the pipeman's detriment. And it's not just the Danes and Germans but also Dutch and American tobaccomen. Confound them!

So would you prefer paying for and smoking pure tobacco or the casings and locked-in moisture that you get with highly processed aromatic tobaccos? Danish blends typically contain as much as 35 percent of the stuff; American blends as high as 25 percent; while the English ones, what few of them remain, less than half of one percent by weight (a purity law for them). "It should always be pure and free from added flavoring, an expedient which is resorted to far too commonly nowadays, probably in many instances to cover an inferior quality of tobacco" (*New York Lancet*, No. 11, 1898).

Now, not all aromatics are created alike. Many of today's craft tobacco blenders eschew the fake and turn out a respectable aromatic with flavors ranging from apricot to whiskey that smell and taste as indicated, though, again, much of the stuff is cloying. I don't blame them as they have a business to run with a large part of that business being pipemen who are conditioned to prefer aromatics. Such pipemen—deserving of the title still—are, sadly, living a life of artificial-sugar-coated gooeyness. But there's hope for even the most mired of our brethren, and it is the duty of every pipeman among us who has seen the light of tobacco purity and refinement to nurture these new and tried pipemen back to the best roots of pipe tobacco smoking: English mixtures.

The probable origin and utter disaster of aromatics is that long ago someone, somewhere, got confused—brilliant, commercially speaking—and said syrup is great on pancakes and breakfast sausage; let's try it in a pipe. And behold it worked or at least that's how it was promoted. Look, if you love maple syrup go to IHOP and order the lumberman's special; if you enjoy three-fingers of rum now and then, I heartily recommend a glass of the dark, fermented juice of the Jamaican cane plant. If your penchant is for a certain food taste, enjoy it as it pleases you but in its classic form, food dish or glass of spirit. Tobacco blenders, this is a plea from all us pipemen: let us taste the bloody tobacco—it's good enough!

Because writing about aromatics is about as distasteful as smoking them, I will end this part by stating that all they're good for is a "hot" mouth and tongue, and a build-up of a sickly cake in the bowl of your trusty pipe. But the choice to switch from aromatics is, of course, yours alone, keeping in mind that your new smoke of pure English or Virginia mixtures will in all likelihood offend those about you.

What sort of tobacco smoker are you?

I've heard from more than a few wise men that there are better tobacco mixtures being sold today than ever before. (I believe this statement has merit, but I disagree with those same people who mark these days as some sort of renaissance in pipe smoking.) If this is true, how does one on a limited budget figure out which mixtures will be right for him?

Wait just a minute. Are you now smoking a mixture that makes you very happy? If you are, then stop. If you prefer consistency and regularity in your life then smoke the same tobacco until you die—boring some will label you, prudent though you would be. "But what of the best tobacco? Ah! does not every smoker know it? It is that which his own soul loves best. In nothing more than smoking does the maxim hold good, 'Chacun a son goût.' One may sing of the rival virtues of pure Virginia, Latakia, Turkish, Cavendish, Shiraz, Golden Cloud, Birdseye, Navy Roll, Rifle Cake, Old Judge, Golden Shag,

Sun-dried, and all the multitudinous forms and qualities of the soothing weed. But each man loveth his own brand or his own blend, and is not to be converted from the belief that it surpasseth in excellence all others." ("Concerning Pipes," *Charles Dickens, All the Year Round. A Weekly Journal*, [London: Chapman and Hall, Third Series, Volume X, July 1, 1893 to December 30, 1893, September 9, 1893], 248). Contrary to what tobaccomen would have you believe, tobacco is not a fashion contest where tastes need changing every so often to keep one in step with the times. Stick with what works for you.

Generally, I recognize two types of pipe smokers. The first is the usually older, probably retired person who has been purchasing the same brand from the supermarket or local tobacconist for his entire adult-smoking life—the Prince Albert or Half and Half guy—but usually the aromatic smoker. The other fellow is younger and is either still trying to figure out what will be his perennial favorite to smoke, or he's someone who sees variety as the spice of life and is forever trying everything new his favorite blenders can scrape together and pack into a two-ounce tin. For this second group the blending houses work overtime.

They have to, because the blenders, boutique small or factory large, are competing for the smoker's business. And if they're not coming out with new blends with regularity, their sales will fade away, because those fickle pipemen are interested in trying the latest and greatest, yesterday's mixture now all too familiar. But if, as I stated in the opening salvo of this chapter, there are but three leaf types, burley, flue-cured Virginia, and Oriental, how many actual unique mixtures are possible? A lot if you read and believe the product labels and published reviews from those professional and amateur tasters.

Of late, reviews of tobacco products for the pipe run profuse, especially online at review-dedicated sites, Weblogs, manufacturers' Web sites, and in the hobby magazines. The quality of the review runs the gamut from philosophical and high-brow bullshit, to the straightforward and simple, to that of the well-learned and knowledgeable taster describing the olfactory aspects detected from each leaf component and who writes with a fair but sometimes boring and woefully uncritical, politically-correct assessment. None of a mixture's reviews will be a substitute for your good taste; nevertheless, they will get you started on a path toward your own discoveries.

Today, far and away the best blenders of aromatics, English, and matured-Virginia mixtures are small, situated in the Unites States, and typically cater to both the discriminating and capricious pipeman. Using three leaf types, they have created ever-evolving lines of mixtures crafted to take advantage of the many flavor nuances derived from leaf varieties and production techniques, some old and some new.

I confess to having a foot in both tobacco camps. I have a few old standbys which I've smoked happily for years and will continue with them for as long as they are made by the same blender in this country, while at the same time I have a mild curiosity for the new and different. So I stumble along trying and throwing away most of what I am given to sample or that I purchase, occasionally coming on to something truly special.

(A superb background to what follows, and because they're both stand-outs as the hobby's quintessential pipeman's guides to tobacco, are two books recommended in chapter 4's reading list: Ehwa's *Book of Pipes & Tobacco*, and Winan's *Pipe Smoker's Tobacco Book*.)

Now, let's take a closer look at the better mixture types.

Virginias

Really good Virginias are the pinnacle of superb smoking for the experienced pipeman and, sometimes, for those with a fire-retardant lining of the mouth. Flue-cured leaf—the heat method by which it is seasoned in the barn and also as it is referred to in the vernacular—is very high in natural sugars, and sugar burns hot, not hot in the temperature sense but in the way it over-sensitizes the delicate surfaces of your mouth. The tobacco is piquant. (English mixtures, on the other hand, are low in sugars and taste cooler.) This is why many prefer smoking well-made or aged Virginias in small pipes along with a slower cadence to their puff. A blender-matured Virginia of, say, three to five years, will have lost a good deal of its sugar bite, and be a regal smoke. I would not disagree with the caution of many experienced pipemen who counsel the curious that this class of pipe tobacco not be taken up by anyone but the attentive and established pipeman.

English

What comprises a good English mixture? For one thing, Orientals (synonymous, more or less, with Turkish), those near-East tobaccos prized for their wonderfully fragrant notes. And, indubitably, as peat reek is to the connoisseur of the single-malt Scotch, Cyprian latakia is to the cognoscenti of the best English mixtures. Latakia is nothing more than a variety of Oriental— Smyrna actually—that is smoke-cured, supposedly using aromatic woods, but the myth of smoldering camel pies probably has some truth to it, at least for the Syrian variety, because I don't believe camels exist in Cypress, whether one-hump or two.

"Too much of anything is bad, but too much of good whiskey is barely enough," said Mark Twain, and I know that many dyed-in-the-wool pipemen feel the same way about their English containing more than enough smoky latakia. It seems that 15 percent will make for a latakia-style blend; 30 percent is huge; but I fancy a few blends using 70 percent: one is full-bodied but pleasant; the other is super tasty but makes me light-headed. I speak of three particularly brilliant mixtures from two of the best blenders this country has ever known: Cornell & Diehl's Pirate Kake mixture (70 percent), and Hermit Tobacco Work's Captain Earle's Nightwatch (30 percent) and Ten Russians (70 percent), the tastiest and strongest English pipe tobacco I know.

Perhaps since the wrist watch became fashionable to quickly tell time, the Englishman has been using a very limited type of what's referred to as condiment tobacco, Perique. And what a lovely, fermented, sweet thing it is. Grown in but one parish of Louisiana, this leaf is a delicious and noticeable addition to many English mixtures in the minutest of quantities. Dunhill's Nightcap is just such a mixture. Not all have it, because some pipemen grow tired of the sweetness and extra heat. I'm one of those. But you simply must smoke and enjoy it for some time for more than just bragging rights—it's a rewarding experience.

Lastly, what is more than a parenthetical note, I will confess that it was only recently I learned that my favorite London-made tobacco, Balkan Sobranie, is composed of Syrian and not Cyprian latakia, as I had always thought. If you read with anger and frustration how Syria acts as a border funnel for terrorists pouring into Iraq to fight our soldiers, then how in Heaven's name can you consider yourself to be a Good Samaritan pipeman by smoking such weed. Smoke the latakia from Cypress, or Greece, it's a far better thing to do and, in my humble opinion, a tastier leaf to smoke. I shall no longer endorse the Sobranie, and will consider it my good fortune that the brand has not been made available for purchase in the United States for many years. God Bless America and Great Britain.

Cross-over mixtures

Are you the fancier of aromatic tobaccos and wish to try or have tried English mixtures and are disinclined to leave the sweetness behind? Then a cross-over mixture is just what the doctor ordered. What I term cross-over from aromatic to English is nothing more—skillfully done, of course—than a mixture of the two, namely black Cavendish, Orientals, latakia and, yes, a sweet tobacco like aged Virginia. A stalwart in this group would include McClelland's British Woods or Frog Morton. This mixture is a welcome change for the pipeman with a sweet tooth.

Today's great variety of mixtures beckons the pipeman, novice and experienced, to experiment along his lines of comfort. For many, their tastes are fickle, with the opportunity to explore each new mixture to hit the tobacconist's shelf a fun game. And, sometimes, his tastiest discovery will be that of a mixture he knows well but one that has seen prolonged aging or, in the argot of the tobacco connoisseur, cellaring, discussed next.

11

Old Tobacco

The young man knows the rules, but the old man knows the exceptions.

—Oliver Wendell Holmes

THERE exists a very small group of dedicated pipemen—and online merchants who cater to them—who regularly turn up long-forgotten sealed tins of tobacco. There may be no better way to waste your money than to buy this old, pricey weed. I will admit not having the chutzpah or interest to ever purchase a can of old tobacco when prices start at $50 for a two-ounce tin and can easily reach into the hundreds, especially for the older and rarer My Mixture Dunhill and Sobranie. From speaking with these brave souls that do, I've learned that the years were either kind on the product or they were not. It's a gamble. Like almost all processed foods, tobacco is a consumable meant to be enjoyed by someone in the here and now with his blood still flowing, rather than in the hereafter. Conjecture runs rampant on Weblogs and at pipe shows about the affect of vacuum sealing the tin has on marrying the elemental tobaccos, that is, where aging in the tin improves with years ... without cessation. Poppycock! (Prove me wrong. Let me sample your tin of 20-plus-year-old Dunhill 965 and I'll rewrite this paragraph crediting you in any subsequent printing of this book.)

For the tobacco maven among us, I'll temper the above with the following caveat: Virginias behave differently with age. Noted pipe collector, cigar writer, and professional tobacco taster and reviewer, Tad Gage, wrote a seminal piece for the casually interested and the dilettante in the winter 2007 issue of *Pipes and Tobaccos* and titled "Aging Tobaccos." Of particular interest to the lover of English and Virginia mixtures, Gage had this to say:

> Blends with no Virginia tobacco, kept under relatively airtight conditions, will last for many years but will taste pretty much as they did when first purchased. Latakia may become a little less intense, but aging blends with no Virginia tobacco is primarily a way to ensure that you can have a future supply of tobacco you really enjoy. Even a non-Virginia blend will develop over time, and

the flavors and oils will definitely marry. The blend may become smoother or more mellow. However, experience has shown me that while these blends develop, they don't really change in a profound way.*

He goes on to state:

The major element of tobacco aging seems to be fermentation, a term that includes a great many organic and chemical changes. In its broadest sense, fermentation describes any organic or inorganic chemical reaction that breaks down complex organic compounds into simpler substances. For example, fermentation in tobacco, whether it's caused by yeast, other microbes, heat or chemical processes might break down complex starches and carbohydrates into simpler sugars.*

Gage concludes his eight-page dissertation:

I can tell you with relative certainty: 1) that high-quality tobaccos change and develop with age; 2) that the changes are positive and, although the result is not necessarily better than the original freshly tinned blend, just different to a greater or lesser degree; 3) that more air and moisture exchange accelerates the aging process; 4) that a higher degree of pressure on the tobacco influences and may accelerate the aging process; 5) that aging doesn't have a detrimental effect on any blend for at least three years; 6) that moisture loss does not equate to a loss of essential oils or flavor (pipe tobacco can be successfully rehydrated); and 7) that nothing is for certain when it comes to aging pipe tobacco!*

But I'll suppress any additional insult on those who partake in the vintage tin game because, like many lifestyles, pipe smoking can and often does evolve into collecting—a way to surround yourself with things you believe make you who you are and how you choose to establish your existence. The chase and discovery of specific old stuff, tinned tobaccos included, can be a part of that and bring you much joy.

Of course, if you've a mind and are patient, you, too, can make your own vintage tobacco. They call it cellaring and Gage's empirical research would apply even more, because you have more control over the "term" than a vintage tin held by someone else that may have been subjected to, say, extreme storage heat.

Cellaring tobacco

I don't believe saving one's favorite tobacco for protracted periods of time would have the cachet of "cellaring," if that part of the country you're from refers to the space beneath the house as the basement or, worse still, crawl space. Cellaring conjures up crypt-like wine cellars in old stone mansions in

---

* Reprinted courtesy the editor, *Pipes & Tobaccos*

Europe. I have a space beneath my house and my dad has always referred to it as the basement, so that's what I call mine. Being smarter than wanting to store my tobacco in a musty "beneath," I elected just to toss everything into an old chest of drawers, above ground. And if the opportunity presents itself, I do not put on airs as to how I cellar such and such but speak of the "drawers."

My Lady Nicotine was the best piece of pipe-smoker's fiction ever written. This 100-year-old tobacco tin, which pays homage to the storied mixture, is from the estate of Tom Dunn, founder, editor, and publisher of the *Pipe Smoker's Ephemeris*. As grand as Arcadia was purported to have been, how well would it have cellared after a century?

The private cellaring of most tobacco (remember Virginias are the exception) makes about as much sense as buying vintage tinned tobacco. The idea behind cellaring is to age tobacco for longer periods of time because you apparently know so much more than the tobaccomen who've spent the better part of their lives mastering the fine art of producing the very tobacco that is your favorite. I really should discontinue here but I'll plow through.

My idea of cellaring harkens back to the chest of drawers. If I buy too much tobacco for some reason, the surplus will go to the drawers. If my countertop glass and ceramic humidor jars are filled, I'll turn recently acquired pouches or tins over to the drawers. If a visitor to my den of smoking iniquity presents me with a gift tin of a good mixture that seems too pretty to rip into, it falls into the drawers. When the drawers are firmly pushed in, it's dark. What happens to the tobacco there is a mystery. To me, not a whole lot can happen, though on one occasion I discovered mice poop; the tobacco was unharmed! (This observation at least proves the point that quality English blends not only ward off pedestrians but vermin too, and this alone should be reason enough to cellar.)

I have tobacco in that 'ol chest pushing 10 years; I've sampled it, because I was hungry at the time and interested to see how it tasted. In most of these trials the stuff remained true to original form (and I guess I should have been thankful for it). In another case I remember well, a six-year-old mixture, now out of production by its American cult, boutique blender, clearly had deteriorated in latakia oomph. I gathered what few remaining tins I had left and handily disposed of them on eBay to a Frenchman in Paris without the slightest tinge of guilt. Maybe the other tobacco would appeal to him more.

Generally speaking, processed foodstuffs don't improve with age beyond the processor's intended period of maturation. Stocking up on tobacco in anticipation of rampant price increases, outright state-mandated tobacco production cessation, or disease and pestilence, is all well and good, but don't rest easy that all will reappear as you left it, or be better from so many years ago. Honestly, I think fresher is better. But, clearly, and according to the sage Mr. Gage, Virginias can improve.

So take your tins and place them in your own chest of drawers or other secret area, mindful that cooler and darker is better than hotter and brighter. Pouch or bulk tobacco should be transferred to glass canning jars. Should you vacuum seal the canning jars like your mother used to when setting up preserves? Don't waste your time. The tobacco in all likelihood will not change much if there's little air present (again, save Virginias, because of the affects of fermentation on lingering starch content). I like to put in as much tobacco as I can comfortably squeeze into the jar without risk of cracking it. And glass—amber glass if you can find it—is best, because it is virtually impervious.

As one final note, I would, however, strongly encourage you to ask your preferred tobacconist or stateside master blender if he will press your tobacco into cakes. Pressing is really the only way to instantly marry the flavors of the various leaves in a mixture and advance the age and luxuriousness of taste. It need be no more complicated or drawn out than this. *Chacun à son bon goût.*

12

Pipe Preservation

Far and away the best prize that life has to offer is the chance to work hard at work worth doing.
—Theodore Roosevelt

WHEN I was younger I wasn't aware that pipes needed to be cleaned. Then when I got heavy into my pipes, the whole cleanliness thing had taken on a zeal bordering on religion. Now, years on, my friends worry about me for not keeping up like they do and think I should. I clench my pipes between my jaws real tight so they cannot fall to the ground. I have half-a-dozen bottles of pipe alcohol cleaner that I may never use. I let the rims of my pipe bowls grow thick and black with the accumulation of tar. When I'm on the move my briar goes into a pocket to be scratched by odd bits of detritus and at great risk of snapping. I'm quickly reaching the age of 50 and am exhibiting that lack of care typically associated with someone much older with less to lose. It's not that I don't give a shit, but I think I know enough about pipes to care when and where it's needed.

There are plenty of fine pipes out there worthy of strict devotion to preservation at all costs. I have no such pipes and I suspect most pipemen don't either. Pipes were never meant for any other purpose than to have a match put to them. There are those pipemen who swaddle their pipes in chamois; they always hold them in their hand while smoking so they need not be held in a clenched jaw at risk of indenting the mouthpiece; and they're forever fussing about cleaning and polishing them as if it were an investment that needed protecting. With super high-end briars selling for more than $750, these pipemen are prudent fellows. But I'm not one of them.

If you're like me and still have a mortgage to pay and a kid to put through university, or are feeling tired keeping up with pipe preservation, take a deep breath. I have some advice for you to take the stress and chore out of being a supposedly conscientious pipeman, next.

Keeping up appearances

1. Pipes, like tobacco, are consumables. If it breaks fix it or have it fixed or throw it out.
2. Clench your pipe with your jaws. Healthy tooth marks are your imprint and safeguard to "dropsy."
3. A pipe is best laid to rest in a pocket while on the go.
4. You should use a minimum of four pipe cleaners as you smoke through a bowl of tobacco. Doing so will offer you a cleaner and tastier smoke, and will make it unnecessary to take-down your pipe as frequently to clean out that troubling gap at the shank's mortise.
5. It is only acceptable to knock your pipe against an ashtray if you derive enjoyment from getting people's attention. Among pipemen it is a serious faux pas, so read your audience carefully prior to attempting such pipe drama. Knocking equates to dinging and knocked-up wood leaves a bad impression.
6. They don't make good vulcanite anymore. Nobody knows why. The stuff just oxidizes so fast it's disheartening. The strangeness of it all is that there's just one firm making the stuff, the Hamburger Company, and it's German, which typically equates with superb engineering and craftsmanship. An oxidized mouthpiece ain't so bad as many exacting collectors make it out to be. How some pipemen get so bent out of shape with this stuff is amazing when their own health is deplorable. Light discoloration is okay in my book, but the heavy-layered whitish-green build-up is unsavory to see and taste and must go. Don't bother trying to rub or buff it out yourself; there are much better things to do with your life. For about $15 a pipe there are enough pipe repair and restoration guys who'll do it for you.
7. Broken shank? I've used Elmer's glue; they say it should be stronger than the wood itself, and I would have to concur.
8. Broken or worn-out mouthpiece? Don't make it a DIY job this time around. Better hand this one to a professional pipe restorer. He'll either cut you a new one, or better still, build up the chewed-up surface to its former self for $25.
9. Pipe bowls split because the wood had a natural fault or because you're smoking too hot. There is no recourse with such failure. Even so, I have a few patent-era Dunhills with splits that carry on with a greater sense of duty than appearances. It would be a shame to retire such faithfuls.
10. Keep your pipes out of bright light and damp environs. It's no good for the wood or hard rubber bits. At the same time allow for some ventilation or your pieces could turn foul-smelling.
11. A steady hand with your lighter or match will save yourself the embarrassment of smoking a pipe with a charred rim.

12. Pipemen will love regaling you with the importance of a proper "cake." The build-up of cake along the walls of the pipe bowl is indicative of a pipeman who smokes regularly. (If there was Scouting for pipemen, this would be the merit badge—the Cake Badge—which they would have their wives sew onto their sleeve.) It does add flavor to a smoke but can sometimes detract. I keep mine dime-thin; more does nothing but restrict bowl capacity.

13. Smoke your pipe slowly and away from a draft. It will smoke better, that is, slower and cooler, with no chance of the wood catching fire.

14. I've never fretted about smoking someone else's cast-off or antique-ish pipe. Older, used pipes, if well cared for, are typically the zenith of pipe smoking as far as I'm concerned, particularly English briars from the 1950s and '60s. I'll remove all trace of the previous owner by cutting out all the accumulated cake with the best pipe-bowl reamer ever made, British Buttner. At that point, you're as close as you're going to get to smoking a new but well broken-in pipe. With a calabash you can't remove the accumulated build-up by cutting it; but you can and should do your utmost to dissolve what you can by using a high-proof spirit of your choice.

15. The easiest preservation is no preservation at all. If you're the pipeman who can't bear the thought of spending more than the cost of a fast-food lunch for the family on a new pipe, do the legion of pipemen who labor through antique malls in search of a find a great favor and junk your old pipes when you retire them. There are too many woebegone pipes filling these knick-knack shops far into the next millennium that no one will or should ever purchase, let alone rejuvenate to smoke again. Parenthetically, the Englishman, as a rule, does not bother with someone else's pipe jetsam, but I think they are missing the boat as the finer, well-kept pieces go. And even then, there are those who feel that almost any pipe can be brought back from the throes of death, even the cheap drugstore stuff.

16. The über-collector has it backward: pipes don't need preserving, pipemen do. So start thinking more about how to care for your body and soul than about the polish on your pipes. Exercise the mind by reading; condition the body by going to the gym; fuel your body with fresh, unprocessed foods; and smoke, as necessary, to bring everything home right.

13

The Collecting Obsession

I didn't play at collecting. No cigar anywhere was safe from me.

—Edward G. Robinson

TWO pipes does not a collection make. Not 10, not 20, or tubs full of them; unless, of course, absolute accumulation is the goal. When I was doing research for my book on the history of the calabash pipe, I bought lots of this pipe type to learn from, but I wasn't collecting them. I had gathered up quite a number of them, but my reasons for doing so were for more than the material object. In the end, the book was published, and I was relieved; I could now stop acquiring them. They languished in my drawers for some time. I had a considerable amount invested and figured I should get it back. I considered selling the lot, but in the end I think I did the right thing by putting them up against the wall to look at. It was three-dimensional artwork, and the visitors to my den admire their beauty, even though they prefer the briar. They liked my collection!

In one definition of the term (I feel its purest and noblest), collecting must have direction and purpose: "To bring together esp. in accordance with a principle of selection or an informative or profitable end" (*Webster's Third New International Dictionary, Unabridged*, 1967). The collector who collects with passion but without regard to any specific theme is a packrat who will pass a wasted opportunity. Those pipemen who suddenly realize after years of enjoying their lifestyle that they've amassed a lot of pipes have an accumulation, but not a collection.

The collector, that person who has clearly defined the objective of his buying and selling activities, can be a powerful—and dangerous—force. What begins as a benign interest sometimes evolves into scary addiction where time and money are spent with reckless abandon. Then again, many of the world's finest museums had their start from the bequeath of one fanatical old man.

This was the case for many museums that contained impressive pipe collections. Today, smoking is pretty much taboo, and you'll rarely find a collection on display in the States, though things are better in Europe. The other issue is lack of exhibit and on-site storage space. Sometimes one will come across shards of clay pipes that form part of a broader display and exhibit theme. And rare is it to see briar pipes on display. This is too bad, because many of today's best living collectors of briar pipes may or may not ever be able to see their life's work set aside for posterity, for all who have an interest to see in some local or out-of-town museum.

The British Character. A Passion for Forming Collections.

You should have no incentive to become a pipe or tobacciana collector, other than an inquisitiveness to learn and a passion for the hunt, because there is no investment value in pipes unless you're looking for a zero-gain return and poor liquidity. And, let me be clear to you on this truth: you don't need to collect to be a pipeman—one pipe can be enough. (You've read in earlier chapters that a pipeman is more than just the sum of his briars.) Many at the pipe shows or Web chat-rooms will clearly be collection-driven. Most throw good money after bad because they got the bug. Resist the urge to follow the herd. Being just a pipeman has always been and can be enough for the majority of men who ever puffed their way through life.

But if you're the collector type with a penchant for the old and uncommon, beware: as a general rule of thumb, and contrary to the seller's bombast clichés of rare, unique, or one-of-a-kind, pre–this or post–that production or "family" era, there really are few truths as to the paucity of briars out there in that great Internet yard sale of eBay. Production numbers were never published by the manufacturers; factory records were never kept or were long ago destroyed by war or the firm. Just because a popular seller makes a statement as to scarcity and value does not make it true; and not infrequently, the online market is not the best guide either, as pipes are not necessarily sold into efficient markets like Wall Street where, it seems, supply always meets demand. The same can be said of a seller/collector of reputation who clearly specializes in briar, but I would tend to believe his cant more. I have been purchasing online for 10 years and, applying a modicum of prudence, I have never been screwed by a pipe e-tailer. Remember, though, their interest is not selfless, so again, caveat emptor.

Now, the exception to this rule is a class of English-made briars that is scarce. These are the pieces roughly between the 1890s and 1930s, the crème de la crème from the only country that produced a substantial and lasting quantity.

Extraordinary or ordinary, old or new, mint or heavily crusted from years of use and abuse, collect what you choose, spend what you dare, but please do it with a plan and a goal and you will succeed. And, maybe, if you're still around and able to comprehend while afflicted with poor health, someone will take a fancy to what you did and tip his hat to you.

Chances are rather good that what you decide to collect will have a dearth of authoritative printed information on it, hence an inability to build your collecting knowledge. Through my own self-discovery of the calabash, with each careful acquisition I was able to deduce incrementally more of my pursuit. It will take years—I think at least five—but at some juncture you will have deduced a pattern and you will be regarded as an authority on the subject.

If you reach such a pinnacle in your collecting world it is your duty, no, it is your debt to everyone who contributed over the years to your success, to give back the knowledge you acquired and in a form better than you discovered it. This can mean one of several things: writing a paper or booklet on the subject; exhibiting the collection; and giving a live presentation at a major convention. Random accumulation of things is a costly and shallow pursuit. The virtuous pipeman will complete the circle of benevolence by giving back in his own way to perpetuate his breed.

Today's pipeman should reflect on this. Pipe extravaganzas, like Chicagoland—a choice way to disseminate information—held regionally or nationally, need more exhibiting. I think there's a wealth of pipe and tobacco knowledge out there in the smoking hinterlands that never sees the light of day. That's too bad but certainly not unalterable. So consider yourself an exhibitor and your collection an exhibit when you're secure with your knowledge of your collection.

A collection or an accumulation? The author chose to decorate rather than sell.

So what plans have you prepared for yourself? Will you become a collector of some repute? Will you be content to travel through your pipe life acquiring pipes willy-nilly? Regardless of the road you choose, be conscious of the very real trap that every pipeman falls prey to. I speak of the "my-favorite-new-pipe" trap. Others have said it before me: you don't need more than a dozen briar pipes to keep you happy. To this, I would add a calabash, a clay, and a meerschaum. That's 15 pipes. Far too many pipesters have this knack of uncovering fantastic pieces—at least for them—that they cannot be without. Well, smoking can only be done one at a time, so in the end the old favorites end up languishing on the rack far removed from the regular rotation. If you find that you're buying more pipe racks, then *you* have fallen prey to the my-favorite-new-pipe trap. To keep things sane and your bank balance on the credit side of the check register, consider selling off the old dead wood. The call of the day is to organize and simplify! Don't leave a mess for your widow to deal with or your pipes will end up in the rubbish bin. Of course, for the true pipe collector, the dilemma is far greater.

14

On the Tobacco Road

I read numerous books—loads in fact—and, as I always do when recording a historical project, immersed myself into the subject matter. I spent many hours at Henry's old homes, such as Hampton Court, and visiting the Tower of London. I read no other books during that period.

—Rick Wakeman

IT is unnecessary for the typical pipeman to be the pragmatic sort. While the practical man can and does often lead a straighter course through life, an existence would be unbearable without those men of the pipe who are happy-go-lucky. I am both, depending on the plan, and associate well with either. Regardless of his soul type, the pipeman is a considerate traveler. While fewer trips or journeys these days are pipe-themed—they can be—after the purpose of a trip is established, the pipeman must contemplate how his travel away from home will impact the ability to smoke his briar. Traveling with your pipe makes every outing a special occasion.

Just as he will contemplate which clothing to pack in his valise, he will devote equal thought to which pipes, tobacco, and pouch to bring along. He will consider both with whom he is traveling and where they will spend their evenings. As the length of a trip extends, so too do the logistics. For instance, a trip to the park for a walk with the dog is a simple matter: a single pipe, perhaps even pre-filled so you can dispense with the pouch. A weekend getaway with the wife to a B&B? This will demand an overnight bag, knowing in advance the smoking rules of the establishment, and the preparation of two pipes. Then there is the business trip to another city or even out of the country. Shuttling between clients and the hotel, how will you manage with a pipe? Is smoking a pipe in the hotel lounge verboten? Perhaps a special moment has arrived—say, an anniversary—and the decision is a week-long Caribbean cruise. Of this last one I have recent and intimate knowledge. It was my parents' 50th-wedding anniversary and a cruise with the clan was in order. I approached the cruise-line well in advance of sailing and asked about its smoking policy aboard ship. I couldn't fathom being pipe-less for such a time. I was tickled to learn that among such other things as a climbing wall, disco, ice-skating rink, and shopping plaza, our vessel included a sumptuous, dimly-lit cigar lounge. It was a brilliant cruise and, for me at least, there was absolutely no need to stop at any of the little islands to get burned under the hot sun while I had my lounge.

To ensure a successful trip, the pipeman must plan for those moments that demand time for a pause and a smoke. And while perfect planning is easily laid to waste, the better the plan, the more that will hold up to the vagaries of life. Basic stuff such as what to bring and knowing the smoking rules are just the beginning. Consider this: each destination will have its secret, unadvertised places where the pipeman can derive pleasures designed especially for him. The tobacconist at the same location for 50 years; a not-too-far-drive to a country-store-type museum with a display of corn cob pipes and tobaccos of the day; a jazz bar just around the corner from your hotel with a wide-open smoke policy; or, perhaps, a special piece of country off the interstate that traverses tobacco fields and leaf-curing barns. It's all there for you to discover. However, advance research about the trip will help map out your free time to devote to such tobacco-related pursuits.

Parks and gardens are my favorites. In fact, any place that the pipeman wants to get to is the right place to be with his pipe. When together with my wife, Priscilla, she'll do the shopping and I'll do the smoking … outside. If she wants me to pop in to look at something she's found, I'll "pocket" the pipe or stick it somewhere outside where it will be safe, such as a window ledge or gate, ready for me to carry on puffing on the return.

I suggest that such planning involve a casual site survey of the area at your favorite Internet search engine, calling shops and museums ahead of time for their hours and, without fail, an email or snail-mail to a pipe-smoking friend or acquaintance to plan a rendezvous. And, what could be most enjoyable, an investigation of any local-area pipe club as to its meeting night.

Unlike the pipe-smoking pals I travel with, I have a preference for packing clothes-heavy and pipe-light. I carry not the pipe purse. (In fact, I tease those who do. If we did not love each other as brothers of the pipe they would most certainly be offended by my remarks about their pipe luggage, but they put up with my nonsense.) The pipes I take are usually packed in a disassembled fashion, mouthpiece from briar proper, wrapped snuggly in a velvet Crown Royal bag. Tobacco is in a large leather roll-up; no tins; two tampers because I always expect to lose one of the little things; and two boxes of wooden matches (lighters can fail at the most inopportune time or, as I've learned from the FAA, are capable of exploding).

Traveling with my pipe, I am never alone. The lone pipeman is a relic. That suits me just fine.

15

Cavendish

Where there is mystery, it is generally suspected there must also be evil.

—Lord Byron

CAVENDISH tobacco, after all of these years of smoking, remains a mystery to me, both what it is and why pipemen carry on with it. I wrote at length on aromatic tobaccos in chapter 10, Cavendish taking the starring role, but I had come to the realization close to a year after writing the piece that my work was incomplete, that there was more damage left for doing on this historical and rightly maligned adulterated leaf. Indeed, enough to warrant an entire chapter. I have been supported in this belief by many erudite pipe smokers who agree as I do. And I have received near equal exposure to fine and well-meaning fellows who believe I have acted silly in my irreverent behavior towards their preferred weed of choice. It is to this latter group that this chapter is dedicated. I can think of not one pipeman I dislike but many whom I disapprove of for they cannot see things my way. With such a bent, I imperil my reputation by no small amount as I must take exception to both Dickens and Twain, both of whom who thought that one's choice was sacrosanct and beneath no one other's; however, they lived too long ago where I could be in a setting of physical harm. And, you may know, tobacco was decidedly different back in the 1800s. True, it was often adulterated with a plethora of non-tobacco ingredients, but oh so different than what science and the artful blender have concocted more recently.

These are my words alone, true enough, yet believe in me that I relish none of the attention for it, for I had hoped after all of these years of smoking that someone braver than me would have come forth to expose the truth. Ah, truth in taste! What, pray tell, can that be? Simply stated, just because you like Cavendish mixtures signifies that while you have taste—we all have that— there is no implication that you have *good* taste. You may see an argument developing rather quickly here; I don't. I may be cheeky, but I am no whack-job—faculties intact.

Every day we deal with the issues of our existence. We read about them in the papers or view them online and, rarely anymore, watch them on the television at six and again at eleven. Our politicians argue the points of the issue convincingly, both for and against. The common man, be he democrat or republican, red or blue, is often left unsure as to the position he should take. Rarely can a position not be softened in one way or another to fit one's political party or point of view. I'm a republican and wish to have the second amendment upheld but think our party's argument on automatic weapons is weak. I am pro life, but I think government should stop itself outside of a woman's vagina. And what about tobacco? I will restate my views cited in preceding chapters: I believe pipe tobacco is pro life but should not be "auromatic!"

What is Cavendish? Maybe like many of you who have read so much about this product that from time to time you hesitate to discuss its properties with other pipemen, or—the horror—its merits, because you have forgotten its finer points, and so you may need a refresher. It would be a far, far easier thing to simply end the discussion, drop the matter, and move on to more palatable topics, but an argument is underway and there are too many souls hanging in the balance, too many pipemen who can be saved. I was once of that group. There was no one to guide me; there was no tobacconist in my community to counsel me; so what the clerk at the corner store had is what I smoked—and he knew as much as what was written on the wrapper, but I'm sure he never read the wrapper. (God only knows how I evolved into the knowledgeable pipeman that I am today.) And so it was Borkum Riff Cherry Cavendish on which I laid my pipe-smoking foundation. The love affair lasted for years. And I remember that my smokes were always "wet" and my tongue was always well bitten. But I simply adored the aroma of that moist-in-the-pouch tobacco and so did those about me.

Proceeding in an historical fashion, we must ask not what *is* but *who* was Cavendish. It would be clean to fix blame on an individual, but, sadly, this cannot be the case. According to Raymond Jahn (*Tobacco* Dictionary, 1954), Sir Thomas Cavendish (1560–c. 1592) was a captain of the Queen's Navy, who, on some famous journey to Virginia in 1585, brought tobacco to England. There are those who claim that he soaked tobacco in sugared water, perhaps to preserve it. According to Carl Weber (*The Pleasures of Pipe Smoking*, 1965), an alternate family member was responsible for the discovery: Lord William Cavendish, First Duke of Newcastle-Upon-Tyne (1592–1676). While Robert K. Heimann (*Tobacco & Americans*, 1960) wrote that the name is attributable to a Norfolk tobacco exporter who prepared his tobacco for the long transoceanic voyage by curing it with licorice. That it wasn't a Dane or a Dutchman may come as a surprise to many who may think of "sweet" tobacco as part of the national identity of those countries if not a small part of its manufacturing heritage.

Yet history books alone cannot lay sole claim to the perplexities surrounding Cavendish tobacco. As to the *what is* Cavendish tobacco, we are again faced with a range of definitions. Weber refers to Cavendish as a distinct tobacco variety that may or may not be processed with sweet flavoring agents. He goes on to state that Virginia and Maryland tobaccos can be similarly processed and be called Cavendish. Robert F. Winans (*The Pipe Smoker's Tobacco Book*, 1977) writes that Cavendish is not a type but a process. Ask someone who purchases his tobacco at Safeway or Piggly Wiggly for the answer. They will have been buying their Amphora, Borkum Riff, or Prince Albert there for decades and should know. They won't. Query several pipemen at the club, they should know. But there will be three different responses each bearing the hemming and hawing typical of one who is unsure, though there will run the undercurrent of a theme that Cavendish is a sweetened tobacco or that it is an aromatic. Then are Cavendishes aromatics?

Few realize that blenders sometimes refer to the way a tobacco is cut also as Cavendish!

All of the above is true, nevertheless, no matter how one cuts the definition or, indeed, the tobacco, it is almost all bad. Who ever fell upon the idea of sweetening tobacco leaf is of less concern to us here than how the pipeman is to deal with what is truly an inexact term. I'll prattle on a while longer because there is actually a Cavendish that is a cut above the rest and one worthy of your attention. It is black Cavendish.

Black Cavendish tobacco is cased or uncased base burley or Virginia tobacco that is steamed under pressure. The process blackens the leaf and brings out the leaf's natural sugars, Virginia, in particular. This type of "Cav" is often used in those delectable hybrid or crossover mixtures for the pipeman who wishes sweetness from his normally dry English mixture. A cautionary note: a burley black Cav will be cased with some sweet nonsense that will foul your mouth and pipe. So if that sweet smelling English mixture never seems to dry out in the pouch, is difficult to light, and smells like rum or cherries jubilee or other similar unnatural odor not associated with a proper English or Balkan mixture, steer clear, it will be your ruin.

I have decided that if there is a calling for a third edition of *Confessions*, that I will say no more on the topic of this style of mixture. Heresy aside, the old saw of how you can lead a horse to water but you can't make him drink, is as true and applicable to a pipeman's tastes as anything else. Just as the horse will eventually drink the water so too will the curious pipeman of good taste reach out for a better refreshment.

16

The Pipe Club

*It is one of the blessings of old friends that you can afford to be
stupid with them.*

—Ralph Waldo Emerson

THE pipeman needs a place where he can hang his hat. His home may
be his castle but even there he may be an unwanted body. The club is
at least a refuge: a monthly destination where he can come in from the
cold and smoke safely, legally, joined by other so pipe-afflicted fellows. All
month long the pipeman will have smoked his pipes and favorite tobaccos in
solitude, foreseeing that one special evening each month when he can immerse
himself in the world of Smokedom with fellow enthusiasts.

But such a time and place is not for every pipeman. It's been my experience
that club life is not for all smokers: he must be willing to socialize. There are
regulars and irregulars—truthfully, all pipemen are irregular—and still others
who do not make a return visit. The pipeman can be a solitary figure. The dare
for every pipe club, then, is to be as welcoming as possible so that the pipeman
who's been smoking a lifetime, and who never knew of the existence of such
things as pipe clubs, can add a whole new dimension to their habit.

Almost a decade ago, three complete strangers met on the Web and
conspired to pool their interest in pipes and tobaccos to form a club. What was
fashioned has evolved into one of my greatest life successes. As a co-founder
of the Seattle Pipe Club, I took the responsibility, along with the astute
guidance of very dear friend and co-founders Matt Guss, Ron Butler, and Al
Ford, and others to design a pipe-smoking club in an image we had fashioned
from nothing. It wasn't hard but it was work—steady work—that no one else
was able or interested to do. Today, the club is widely acknowledged as the
archetype of what a pipeman's club ought to be, in a city not celebrated for its
pipemen. Clubs at Boston, Chesapeake, Chicago, Columbus, Kansas City,

New York, Philadelphia, Richmond, Sacramento, Washington, D.C., say hello to Seattle!

Just as two pipes don't make a collection, neither does a roof overhead make for a pipe club. The mechanics of a club can be as simple as one chooses to design. If my name was going to be associated with a club it would have to be special. Consequently, added to the roof we made certain we had four walls, heat, plenty of snug seating, a full bar with a  kitchen to serve short fare, and an ambiance that would make us all feel blessed to be alive and amongst friends who would come to know why the pipe was such a wonderful thing.

For a variety of circumstances, our fast-growing club would come to uproot and move to new addresses every few years. But we stuck collectively. The bonds of the pipe and our comradeship were strong. But there was something more that kept the boys coming out. And here's the rub: if what you want for your club is a wide and varied allure, the experience must be beyond the length of the pipe to other goings-on.

The club's steering committee did its volunteer best to always have a show prepared. We realized, even as we planned for that first meeting, that the members wanted to have something unfold in the haze of their smoke. That show was different each month and included an eclectic range, such as fly-fishing outfitters, pipemakers and master tobacco blenders, brewers and distillers and vintners, book writers and war storytellers, single-malt Scotch tasting, psychologists, medical doctors, U.S. Navy SEALs, pipe rejuvenators, caricaturists, et cetera.

The point is, we did our level best to broaden the educational and entertainment horizons of the membership because, quite frankly, all pipe and no play makes Jack Pipeman a dull boy.

A pipe club can do more, like slow-smoke

TUCOPS. The mother of all pipe clubs is no longer.

competitions, annual dinners and auctions, have a presence on the Worldwide
Web, summertime barbecues, road trips to neighboring state and provincial
clubs, but it must have an element that not many clubs have: a leader. A leader
never volunteers for the job; he's just there and assumes control out of chaos,
acting as a kind of benevolent dictator. Leadership, or lack of it, will make or
break a club. It is the singular thing clubs either have or have not. And not just
someone who will get things done—that's important—but a pipeman with the
wherewithal, vision, and stick-to-itiveness to get it on for the long haul.

There are many clubs that do less. They gather to eat and drink and smoke,
present and swap their pipes and tobaccos, and tell stories or describe with
relish upcoming pipe travels, and everyone is content with such status; that's a
fine deal. My club did things differently. All I can tell those interested in
building a new club or changing the direction of a tired one, is to build it the
way you envision it, and to nurture a treasury so you can afford to do things.
And don't expect anyone to pitch in to carry the load … they rarely do. It's
lonely at the top.

A contingent from the Seattle Pipe Club descends on Chicagoland 2007.
(*Left to right*) Milt Strasburg, Al Ford (club auctioneer), Greg Hampton, Craig
Watness (U.S. slow smoke time record holder), the author, Tom Wolfe (club
photographer), Joe Lankford (club master blender), Dr. Henri Gaboriau (club
physician), and Matt Guss (the club's "really smart" treasurer).

That said, the interest in pipe clubs ain't what it used to be. Go figure. If you reside far from a large city, the prospect to pal around with other like-minded men is, sadly, remote, but all is not lost! These days, it seems that more pipemen partake in the virtual club from the sanctity of their home communing in online smokers' forums. I've tried a few, such as *Pipes & Tobaccos'* Foundations. They can be fun, instructive, and an easy means of introduction to other pipemen you might someday be able to meet at a show. I often find many of the "threads" are absolute drivel. See for yourself. I suppose some may find virtual companionship better than none.

17

Your Place to Smoke

Home is a name, a word, it is a strong one; stronger than magician ever spoke, or spirit ever answered to, in the strongest conjuration.

—Charles Dickens

WHERE do you smoke your pipe? To make it less awkward for you to answer this question, allow me to do it for you: outside! "Despite its rich history, pipe smoking is now an affectation best savored privately, where your friends won't notice that you look like a parody of a Norman Rockwell painting—or that your favorite 'blend' smells like a fire at a Log Cabin Syrup plant" (Sam Stall, Lou Harry, and Julia Spalding, *The Encyclopedia of Guilty Pleasures: 1,001 Things You Hate to Love*, [Philadelphia: Quirk Books, 2004], 208–209). Obviously, it used to be that you could smoke everywhere, even in a hospital bed in between breaths of oxygen. But the anti-smoking tide started turning long ago such that just about all tobacco smoking is verboten. And in this author's opinion, it has been the mother of all "anti" tides. So, not inside any government building; not inside a public building (newly defined to mean privately-owned establishments especially if there are employees); not within private clubs (technically public as now loosely defined, but not open to the public because, well, it's private); not in restaurants or bars; not on the beach or beachside sidewalk in Del Mar, California (I can attest to it, I was there!); not in airplanes, trains, or your automobile in Washington State if your passengers are minors; and not in your home proper because you've recently elevated your smoking tastes to include English mixtures, and your wife will have none of it. So we're back to the garage or outside. Perhaps this chapter should have been called *Concessions of a Pipeman.*

Maybe it's not as bad as that for you. Maybe what you have is a carport or portico. Maybe it's the deck or back patio where there's a sun umbrella or awning that you can use when it's raining. Things could be decidedly different if you're holed up in an apartment or condo. Here, all you might have is a balcony but only available when the neighbors have their windows and sliding door shut.

What? You say you can smoke within your own home? If you're not a bachelor, divorced, or recently widowed, it means you're sharing your space with one whose respect you should continue to garner, because you are especially fortunate to be pitied and taken in from the cold.

"This is Norman's little bureau of alcohol, tobacco, and firearms."

They say the pipe is the great consoler. If this is true, you pipemen who have been banished to the outdoors when you'd rather be indoors, will need all the help your pipe can offer you. You may not believe there's much you can do by yourself when you're facing state laws or city anti-smoking ordinances —and you're probably right. But we live indoors where the government has no say. And home is the best place to smoke. So if you're currently in the doghouse—literally or figuratively—sort out what you need to do to get back where it's comfortable and where you and your pipe can get down to serious smoking.

Before I get on telling you what to do to create that perfect home setting for you and your pipe, remember this: by smoking a pipe or cigar you are not acting selfishly to those around you. Perhaps you're inconsiderate by not dealing with the smoke and smell, but those issues can be tackled in a sensible way if one has a mind to it. As you must now be acutely aware, there's much more to the smoking of a pipe or cigar than the material. And because so much is at stake, I would prefer that you not take anything for granted. Therefore, I believe it needs spelling out to those about you at home whose wit is, to put it kindly, one dimensional on the topic of smoking. So, when the mood is absolutely perfect, and your wife or life partner has their defenses at bay, read this passage to them.

> The man dragging nervously on at a cigarette, he argues, can hardly rise above the petty problems and tensions of the world. But in the aromatic blue haze of the clear Havana, or the mellow smoke curling upward from the seasoned briar, a man can aspire to greatness; can see the way, perhaps, to unravel the tangled skein of domestic and international problems. ... Ladies especially, should not confine their thinking on the cigar and pipe to such trivialities as smelly curtains and ashes on the rug, but should cling to this thought: That which makes a man more mellow, that which can calm him and raise him above himself, must, perforce, make the world a better place. ("Cigars & Pipes—In Style Again," *Changing Times, The Kiplinger Magazine*, Vol. 14 No. 12, December 1960, p. 45.)

When you *arrive*, you must claim your space and that may also include time slots when you're permitted to take your pipe. Regardless, give due consideration to what's needed for perfect pipe relaxation. First and foremost, you must give due thought to the smoke. If you fail to adequately deal with it you won't get very far with your wife or life partner. For the price of several modestly priced briars, you can get a quality air purifier that will work wonders. I recommend the Friedrich C-90B Electronic Air Cleaner, an electrostatic affair that as of this printing has the best consumer ratings for filtering smoke. Size the unit correctly for the cubic footage of your space. And if your space is too large for you to be given free reign, consider erecting a partition wall.

The author's smoking den.

Your next thought should be towards décor. I'm not expecting you to have decorator genes, but forethought to atmosphere adds measurably to the smoking experience. Show your wife that you're serious about your objective, and that pipe smoking is not something that can or should be relegated to the garage. Any Tom, Dick or Harry can plop himself down into his La-Z-Boy with a beer and a cigar and think that it couldn't possibly get any better. Well, for the pipeman, it can and it should. With some interest, knowledge, and a little planning, one can truly create the best smoking den in the neighborhood. Your selection for a room theme should certainly be based on your varied interests. Like mine, it could be based on the realm of smoking and reading. But your choice may be fishing, hi-fi or high-definition TV with surround sound, or NASCAR, where pipes and tobaccos play a secondary theme.

Other than a smoke-eating machine and your favorite chair, there are no hard rules to the design of your space. But consider the following:

1. You spend considerable time and money selecting your pipes. You should spend no less in the design of your premises and its furnishings.
2. Having a room designed especially for your leisure pursuits will also be of interest to your like-minded pipe-smoking friends, and will afford you the opportunity to entertain in a style befitting the classiness of the pipeman.

3. It seems that being a pipeman means that before long you will have acquired all sorts of pipe requisites that have cluttered up all available shelf space. Get rid of them. You do need a place to set a drink down, don't you? Alternatively, artistically arranged, well-coordinated or themed stuff, even if packed together tightly, does have the same comforting effect as a sparsely decorated space.

4. Wall hangings are it. Say you have a fondness for old tobacco and pipe magazine advertisements, select your favorites—less is more; have them matted and framed, and hang them on the wall. You may have a clutch or two of old briars that have fallen into disuse that you are unable to part with. Frame them in some geometric arrangement and hang them up. If you're starting from scratch, you should consider the many excellent online picture libraries that offer smoking-themed prints. Select the size you want, they'll frame it and send it to you ready for hanging. I recommend www.maryevans.com and www.punchcartoons.com for a swell array of older images from the heyday of British pipe smoking.

Single- or double-breasted, the velvet smoking jacket exudes elegance.

5. Even with an air purifier, a stale scent will persist if you are unable to ventilate to the outdoors. Your hippie days may be far behind you, but you should consider incense. Smoker's candles don't work.

6. Along with reading a good book, a natural accompaniment to a pipe is a drink. Whether Scotch, port, beer, or ice water, have the necessary items and glassware at hand by conceiving a bar area.

7. A gentleman need no more in his wardrobe than the best single suit of clothes he can afford. With it and the confidence from being a pipeman, there is no more to decorating a room than his presence. He will be watched! And no garment bespeaks the air of the classic pipeman as the quilted velvet and silk smoking jacket. Whether single- or double-breasted, the smoking jacket with traditional silk-cord frogging and shawl collar is the ultimate accoutrement for you at home, whether smoking alone or hosting friends and members of your club for an evening quaffing Scotch and bowls of rich latakia mixtures. The Real McCoy is still being tailored in London and will set you back measurably with prices ranging from £500 to £1000. The paradigm of this classic Edwardian garb can be had at Pakeman, Catto and Carter of Cirencester, England, and at Turnbull & Asser, Jermyn St., London, Beverly Hills, and New York.

8. And, if you do build a smoking den truly grand by today's minimalist smoking standards, do invite your best cigar- and pipe-smoking chums to share in your good fortune, and take pleasure in their envy.

18

The Healthy Smoker

It seems a pity that the world would throw away so many good things merely because they are unwholesome. I doubt if God has given us any refreshment which, taken in moderation, is unwholesome, except microbes. Yet there are people who strictly deprive themselves of each and every eatable, drinkable, and smokeable which has in any way acquired a shady reputation. They pay the price for health. And health is all they get for it. How strange it is! It is like paying out your whole fortune for a cow that has gone dry.

—Mark Twain

HAVING finished writing this book, I was ready to proceed to editing, but I was apprehensive—I was fearful I was leaving something out. As a relatively new author, I can imagine that other writers have this same fear of a seemingly complete work before them only to realize they found a better way to express a point, wanted to reframe the conclusion or, worse, missed something, but it was too late! The book had been published!

I like the juxtaposition of the words 'healthy' and 'smoker,' and, thus, the choice of title for this *almost-missed* chapter. Today, in particular, this chapter title is, unquestionably, quite oxymoronic. But that would depend on your point of view and understanding of the matter, right or wrong on the facts. My other choice for a title was the *Happy Smoker*; I thought it would offend fewer people, but as we're all led to believe, smokers die and they can't be happy about that.

Smoking a pipe is sheer pleasure. Yet for every pipeman there lurks in the shadows of his mind a niggling reminder that not all may be well in his pursuit of pleasure. At first glance, this seems customary and reasonable: shouldn't there be some reservation or guilt balancing this soulful equation? Maybe. It's been drilled into all of us that smoking is harmful to our health and to anyone nearby breathing in our secondhand smoke. Regardless of the truth or falsehood of this last statement, are you at ease knowing this? There was a time when such thoughts occupied my daydreaming. The sore throat after that

Mark Twain was noted for doing at least two things first-rate and profusely: writing and smoking. This *Vanity Fair* illustration from 1908 shows the great humorist, America's father of literature, smoking an English-made calabash at the pinnacle of its popularity.

wonderful party Saturday with friends, smoking the pipe and passing many a fine dram of single-malt Scotch whiskey. Could this be the harbinger of oral cancer?

Private reservations such as those I described are all too real and, I would surmise, also pervade many a pipeman's thoughts from time to time. Such inner questioning is far-sighted. If I thought for a minute that my pipe-smoking lifestyle would end my life prematurely—say, cut short by several years, my larynx removed, or my tongue carved up—I believe I would give up the lifestyle post haste! Yet I don't feel that's the case, so I carry on. But I think there are some pipemen who frequently worry about their health, and this detracts from *their* happy lifestyle. Perhaps it's easier for them to come to terms with their cherished routine by smoking a pipe less often. Ironically, few of us have much choice anymore but to smoke fewer and fewer pipes, given the advanced state of our current anti-tobacco culture, and laws and ordinances aplenty banning smoking in public buildings and most private establishments. Either way, this pall cast upon the smoker, disclosed to you later in the chapter, is wholly unwarranted.

How could smoking a briar be harmful? If the non-smoker who believes everything he reads about the harmful effects of cigarette smoking could only see the pipe smoker for what he is—so much unlike those who indulge in cigarettes with reckless abandon—that person would see a man who is patient, content, relaxed, and at peace with himself and the world around him. Does this not contribute to one's health? But he is unable or disinterested in any view other than that which is constantly in the media … that smoking kills. The assessment is not incorrect in the absolute: smoking does kill. Then again, so do many other pursuits, but no other personal indulgences have similar government restrictions and warnings or public scorn as smoking tobacco.

Under full and accurate disclosure, you should know that recent scientific research on tobacco-related deaths has not just to do with the diseases associated with the cigarette; similar investigation has been conducted on the pipe. Notwithstanding the fact that 100 percent of the anti-smoking rhetoric targets the cigarette, it is true that, years after the U.S. Surgeon General's 1964 report had something kind to say toward pipe smoking[3], the pipe smoker was also studied again, and the results are not encouraging, or so it seems at first glance. But don't be so fast to snuff out your briar. More on this later.

Three things determine one's health: heredity, disposition, and lifestyle. Most of us have the capacity to guide our physical and mental destiny. While there's zilch we can do about our DNA (at least for now), everyone has the opportunity to focus on their personal outlook, and the manner by which they choose to conduct their life. As they say, it takes all kinds, including those who choose that standard of living that embraces the briar.

I believe that as I get on in years I'm becoming wiser—with those close to me quick to include irreverent as an additional character trait. One of my pet peeves, which simultaneously amuses and rankles, are the self-righteous know-it-alls, those of slight character whose intellectual bearing is built on the foundation of the day-to-day news churn. They believe everything they hear, read, and watch in the media, particularly that which proliferates on the Web. Thus, the findings of a research study become gospel, because "science" cannot be misrepresented, and they can understand the simple sense behind it. So, one day red wine is good for your heart, and the next day it's not. Chocolate is also good, because it does this or that to some bodily function, but later it's determined to cause an offsetting malady to another part of the body. How about eight glasses of H_2O each day to keep sufficiently hydrated? Now doctors are reconsidering that notion. Homeopathic remedies? The science has never been validated. The folk who live by this daily regime of oftentimes biased or junk epidemiological research are drowning in a sea of stupidity of their own choosing. These are many of the very same people who clearly have an eating disorder, but select a 32-ounce diet soda in an effort to mind their caloric intake while justifying the extra cheese in their stuffed-crust pizza-pie. It reminds me of the hilarious scene from the 1975 medieval-set movie *Monty Python and the Holy Grail*: peasants were being led to believe, through a series of completely unrelated absurdities, what determined whether a woman was a witch, something about if a stone floated in water or not. Like rocker Lou "Mr. New York" Reed once penned for a song, believe none of what you read and only half of what you see. And so, they would blindly have us believe that all types of smoking and exposure to cigarette, cigar, and pipe,

---

[3] "Death rates for current pipe smokers were little if at all higher than for non-smokers, even with men smoking 10 or more pipefuls per day and with men who had smoked pipes for more than 30 years" (*Smoking and Health: Report of the Advisory Committee to the Surgeon General of the Public Health Service*, 1964, 13).

in any quantity and for any duration, are all the same. Worse than secondhand smoke, that's a lot of hot air! Or as the eccentric magicians Penn and Teller would sound off, bullshit!

Hyping health risks

Today, science is unrelenting and increasingly so sophisticated that it boggles even the trained mind. But behind every science are people, and people are prone to have the same biases and maladies as the man on the street who punches in every day, struggling paycheck to paycheck to make ends meet. What is he to believe of the out-of-context sound-bites that permeate day-to-day living? Is all that information overloading his capability to adequately judge its merits, and is it making him feel bad about how he has modeled his lifestyle? Shouldn't the practice of moderating his consumption of human vices effectively keep him out of harm's way? I believe so, but that will never stop the puritanical do-gooders from pouring on bit after carefully-selected bit of statistical scraps to prove that the evils of smoking are unequivocal. Sadly, the fight to preserve our freedom to smoke about town was lost some time ago. And I am only now beginning to realize why not much of a fight has been waged by the smoker, more particularly, the pipeman.

With the confidence coming from an understanding that most publicized bits of scientific research concerning the moderate pipe smoker is grossly inaccurate and deceptive, you too can learn to relax and puff contentedly, knowing that only good can come of the pipe. The author proves the point, here, in a sitting for his sketch in Leicester Square, London, spring 2008.

As I was doing research for this chapter, much of it was on the relatively crude and young science of epidemiology, or as some have coined it, research by numbers. I had finished reading *Hyping Health Risks* by Geoffrey C. Kabat (New York: Columbia University Press, 2008). I enjoyed it very much and discussed one of the chapters with a co-worker. It was about the controversy over passive smoking, or ETS, environmental tobacco smoke. An educated person, she knew as much about epidemiology as I did prior to reading the book, so I began telling her what it was; this was not our typical water-cooler small talk, I can assure you. When I thought we were ready to move on, I introduced the topic. Before I got very far, she figured out my endgame and began talking me down. Was I naive? Did I actually believe that smoking tobacco was not injurious to one's health? It got progressively worse. I explained to her that I wasn't talking about direct smoking per se, but ETS. That didn't matter to her because it was all the same, all bad. I could plainly see her mind was closed, and simple reasoning would be ineffective to further the discussion. I turned and walked back to my side of the office.

"Don't worry. If it turns out tobacco is harmful, we can always quit."

The topic of tobacco smoke and human disease is pretty ugly, and a discussion on it can be extremely passionate. It seems that everyone knows someone who was afflicted with a miserable end because of smoking.

Cigarette smokers will look at you queerly if you try to paint anything but a picture of craving, dependency and nicotine-addiction when discussing their "fix." Talking dispassionately about the benefits of smoking tobacco these days is about as safe a challenge as running with the bulls in the streets of Pamplona. The truth is that there is no single truth concerning the health risks associated with pipe smoking, but each and every so-called truth is cloaked in the gray matter of study results based on the science of epidemiology.

What exactly is this science? Epidemiology is an observational science of, well, epidemics, that is, diseases that affect large populations as opposed to the single human being. Through statistical analysis, it attempts to study health or lifestyle risks that are causal to multistage chronic diseases. And most important, it seeks to quantify the risk of contracting disease through such behavior. But the science's singular strength is also its Achilles' heel: observational data. If you're old enough to feel comfortable smoking a pipe in public, you're probably of an age to know you can get statistics to substantiate any conclusion you wish to push onto the unsuspecting. Mark Twain knew it when he stated, "There are lies, damned lies, and statistics." He was also reputed to have similarly mused, "Facts are stubborn, but statistics are more pliable." The biases in observational data collection are a real problem for the epidemiologist. So, too, are confounding data from other influences: was that killer heart attack caused by the fact the gent was a smoker, or because of an unknown hereditary condition or fatty diet? But the epidemiologist has techniques for dealing with such influences on his case subjects, like a control group, or so he thinks. And then there's the notion of statistical significance. For instance, say research indicates that smokers who smoke two to four pipes a day are 20 percent more likely to develop cancer of the larynx. Is this significant? Nope. In fact, generally speaking, the health industry regards any relative risk below 2.0–3.0 (i.e., 200–300 percent more likely to contract the disease than the unaffected control group) to be insignificant. This is because of the great difficulty to secure and sample large population groups that are not confounded by unrelated health influences or other commonplace sampling errors.

But this is for the anti-smoking lobby to know and for you not to find out. But now you know! Fact is, the "anti" lobby groups regularly place disproportionate emphasis on the significance of a number, any number, to prove their point that smoking causes disease and kills. Of course, it's absolutely irresponsible, but their agenda is a life or death proposition—accuracy, truth, and science be damned. And, incredibly, slanted studies have appeared in reputable medical journals substantiating these tenuous causal associations, particularly ETS, heart disease, and lung cancer.

So what and whom is the pipeman to believe? And what can he do to be a healthy smoker? Common sense is a good starting point, like moderation, to not inhale, to be physically fit, and to do what makes you feel good. "Less is more, even in smoking. Make it a philosophy. Make it a delightful celebration" (Zino Davidoff, *A Renaissance of Pleasure* [Hamburg: Reemstma International GmbH, 1985], n.p.). While no one need feel trapped next to a smoker's secondhand smoke (and I know the pipeman is considerate of these individuals and smoking situations without making a fuss), no individual or government has the right to limit one's personal freedom and choice to do as he pleases. But there's more helpful advice out there for the pipe smoker who is willing to buck the anti-smoking trend, with a mind towards the upkeep of his health and his pipe-soothing lifestyle. An excellent launching point is the Web, in particular, a short but excellent array of articles and links from my home-club's Web site, www.seattlepipeclub.org. Click on Sherlock's Corner and go to Smoker's Health Information.

I tried very hard not to write anything related to disease in this book. The media barrage is depressing, with publicized "scientific" facts, more often bold lies from otherwise respectable, well meaning, credulous people. I have no confessions to expose other than the infrequent reflection that maybe my lifestyle could stand some improvement. Alas, with the busy schedule of a salesman, I concluded long ago that two pipes a day, instead of one, was a hard thing to do!

There should be nothing more comforting for the pipeman than a quiet longing in between his pipes and nirvana when he's actually at it. That the actions of the idiotic and near-sighted have so fucked up the civilized world for the pipeman is a sad reality. There are some who talk of nothing else but tobacco's imminent demise and, along with it, the smoker. They are not incorrect in this assessment. I believe it, for the signs are all around us. And while I see myself as cynical and irreverent, I retain and project an optimistic bearing that carries me through every day, from pipe to pipe. I find it's a much better way to live … however long that may be.

19

Heart of Hearts

If money is your hope for independence you will never have it. The only real security that a man will have in this world is a reserve of knowledge, experience, and ability.

—Henry Ford

DOING the right thing is not always easy. Often, the results can be damaging. Nevertheless, you know instinctively which road is true and beyond moral or ethical reproach, at least for you. But for what should be the simple stuff to decide upon, the steadying hand of common sense is not always around when you need it, so mistakes are made.

Did you ever get the feeling that people didn't want you to smoke your pipe? I mean, apart from all of the anti-smoking messages we read every day, what image do you feel you portray as you walk about town sending out voluminous clouds of smoke in a society so focused on a definition of what is acceptable? Live and let live ain't good enough anymore. Generally speaking, I do not take issue with the rules governing secondhand smoke in enclosed public spaces, namely government edifices. For the non-cigarette smoker, these little sticks of chemically-laced tobacco emit a lingering odor which is utterly revolting. So I have come to favor this country-wide law. Sadly, as we all know it to be, the reality is that initial directive has morphed into the ugly beast of Puritanism that once infected this country regarding alcohol. What common theme both movements have shared is the limiting of free choice. In chapter 18, The Healthy Smoker, I made the case that the foundation for the prohibition of smoking was the intentionally subjective and careless use of statistics through the guise of the pseudo science known as epidemiology. It took a constitutional amendment to extricate the country from the disaster that was prohibition. What will it take to disentangle the pipeman from today's version of the same thing?

But pipes are different you tell those willing to listen. Children don't smoke pipes or cigars like they do cigarettes. You don't inhale when you smoke tobacco through either of these two mediums. (Mind you—and this is never pointed out by pipemen—there is the inhalation of your own secondhand smoke.) Whether or not such an effect can ever be measured accurately to gauge if one is at a significant health risk, would be next to impossible to determine. Even if it could be, who would listen? Mouth and esophageal cancer should be a consideration, but again, enter the concept of temperance and the elevated risk of cancer should be slight, measurably insignificant. Christ, what motor vehicle exhaust one breathes in on a busy street corner while waiting for the signal to change, is surely worse. Nevertheless, at this point in American and European society, the smoker is an easy mark for legislative abuse. At the rate things are progressing, what with one new bill after another becoming law in most states, there may very well come a time when tobacco will be considered a drug to be prescribed by physicians. In all likelihood, the only place one will be able to smoke is within the confines of one's stick-built castle. Still, tobacco could be outlawed completely, unavailable except through the mechanisms of the black market. Smoking is fun enough without running the risk of bootlegging as was the case during prohibition.

In such an inhospitable climate, what is the pipeman to do? I believe there are two things one can and should give careful consideration to; one being a good hedge if the other fails. First, consider having your state change its laws on the right to smoke. Few would oppose the notion that the anti-smoking movement was centered virtually completely upon the cigarette. Relatively speaking, so few men smoke pipes, let alone cigars, that no one cares or should care about them, only in as much as they need to be explicitly excluded from a state's smoking laws. Realistically, the chances you have of garnering support from your two state representatives and senator, are slim to none. They may be smokers themselves, but they would be remiss if they write, sponsor, or vote yes on a bill that is viewed as pro smoking.

But you needn't necessarily attempt to eat the entire elephant in one sitting. I cite the following example. In July 2009, the state of Washington passed Senate Bill 5340 with the following message:

> A person may not ship tobacco products, other than cigars weighing more than three pounds for 1,000 units, purchased by mail or through the internet to anyone in Washington other than a licensed wholesaler or retailer. A person may not, with knowledge, provide substantial assistance to someone violating this tobacco shipping restriction.

The intent was to end sales of cigarettes to minors from out-of-state, typically accommodated by the anonymity of the Internet. I am not a constitutional attorney, but I do know that states cannot interfere in what is clearly a federal matter. Notice, too, that large cigars were exempt. It happened this way because the fat-cat senators, supported by an encouraging cigar-industry lobbyist, wanted their "cake" and the ability to smoke it too! As it turned out, tobacco destined for the pipe was not a consideration, so that by not receiving any mention it—again—was lumped into a new piece of anti-smoking legislation. Apparently, Washington has but one senator who smokes a pipe, and he must not have raised much of a fuss because the bill passed handily.

What I know of the effect of this law, was to make several normally law-abiding citizens and members to my pipe club give serious consideration to disobeying the law by ordering their tobacco online from their e-tobacconist of choice. I gave it consideration in fine Thoreau fashion and decided that my government had over-stepped its authority and was treading where it had no constitutional right.

The state went ahead and began contacting the prominent Internet tobacco merchants to inform them of their new law. I presume the intent was also to intimidate and threaten. I know of one very large New York seller whose attorney took the letter rather seriously and decided to cease all shipments of tobacco to Washington.

Parenthetically, the same nonsense is carried on with alcohol. There are a handful of states that are still so possessed by the repeal of prohibition in 1933 (all states fully repealed the 18th Amendment in 1966), that quite a few still try to dissuade out-of-state shippers from selling directly to consumers. Of course, the matter has just a little to do with uncollected sales and excise taxes. Some of these sellers will not ship into states with such laws, and there are others who could give a rip.

In the meanwhile, pipemen in Washington State were to have a difficult time of it, even with the plucky nature of a few of its club members who decided to take the bull by the horns and get the law amended. Much like the exemption for cigars, surely the legislators were not worried about children purchasing loose pipe tobacco online to smoke in a pipe.

Guess what happened? Early in 2010, one of our club's members was able to convince his senator to sponsor a bill to amend SB 5340, to explicitly exclude pipe tobacco from this new anti-smoking bill. There were hearings—in both houses, where club members including this author gave testimony—but to no avail, for even though we knew the chances to garner enough interest and support for a vote and to emerge from committee for full votes on the floor, the state's attorney general's office—at the time, vociferously anti-tobacco—would have none of it. The bills died. And so, pipemen will be acting feloniously when purchasing their tobacco through the mail from out-of-state vendors. Even though our efforts were met with no success, pipemen in Washington State are at least fortunate they have someone in their corner fighting for their rights. They owe the debt of gratitude to the Seattle Pipe Club for existing and for doing more than what most clubs do and that is sitting around—club-footed!—smoking, griping about legislation they feel they have not the power to change.

House Health Care & Wellness Committee
TVW Webcasting
00:14:15   01:44:04

The author and other members of the Seattle Pipe Club gave testimony at a
senate hearing at the state Capitol in Washington, in an effort to remove the
restriction on inter-state and Internet sales of pipe tobacco.

There's no arguing it: the modern-day pipeman is about the most peculiar type of smoker imaginable. But he need not stand alone in the wilds of civilization. His club can be an excellent support mechanism, but he will find that it is not typically ready and willing. It needs a catalyst for change. But there will usually be men about interested in joining the fight for the common good. Changing the law to side with the pipe smoker is a novel idea. And understanding your state's laws is an excellent way to start. Again, consider the elephant. If you're going to tackle the matter with any hope of success, find the small opportunities, cracks, loopholes, anything, that will get you started. Eventually, you will need to turn to your house representatives and senators to sponsor a bill. Once sponsored, your new bill will run the gauntlet of the legislative process. It'll be a real fight. But I believe a club should have direction. Fighting the bastards that have limited our rights to smoke where and when we chose, to be no better a fight for today's pipeman, to be sure, the only one.

The other notion I've come around to is the idea of stockpiling tobacco. (Not hoarding, for the pipeman is always generous with his weed.) A time may come when tobacco will no longer be available for sale or become prohibitively expensive to purchase. Lardering up on tobacco for such a pipeman's apocalyptic event I think would be a difficult thing to do. Considerations such as quantity, type of mixtures, cost, security, shelf-life, space, etc., all come into play when deciding on such a course.

Consider quantity. How much will you need for the next, say, 25 years? Say your average pipe holds a five gram pinch of tobacco. If you smoke a bowl twice daily, every day, you'll need to stock up on 3.65 kilograms for each year or 91 kilograms on 25 years. That's 200 pounds! At, say, $60 per pound for premium tobacco, you have a stockpile that will cost you $12,000. Heaven help you if you tire of your selection or if it deteriorates within the can or Mylar bag.

If you fancy such a plan and are of the means to make good on it, shop around. A bulk purchase of this magnitude will interest the tobacconist immensely such that he will yield from his usual mark-up.

Hopefully, what you like is available in at least a half-pound-sized can or quality laminate plastic bag. Clear plastic, typically heavy gauge polyethylene bags or "poly," are unacceptable because it permits light and air to pass through, slowly degrading the contents. Repacking in brown glass is an option, but will be a royal pain in the *tuchas* and much heavier to *shlep*.

All the same, you run the very real risk that so many years and bowls into the future, the tobacco has spoiled, it has turned flat, devoid of the feature taste elements that drew you to it in the first place. Frankly, I would not purchase more for than five years out. Sure, five years hence prices will have gone up a little or a lot but hopefully, so too your income.

Retired on a fixed income, or living paycheck to paycheck? Consider establishing an informal co-operative to purchase much larger quantities at wholesale prices. Like-minded health nuts have formed natural and organic food-buying co-ops nationwide. I see no reason why like-minded tobacco fanciers cannot do likewise. Actually, if you already belong to a pipe club, why not flex its muscle and get better pricing. By buying individually, club members act inefficiently. A coordinated purchase by a group will yield surprising returns. For maximum benefit, I suggest semi-annual or even annual meetings where orders can be taken and placed with a single shop or online tobacconist.

On the other hand, the way some of us carry on about vintage tobacco, if you're lucky enough to select a brand of favor 25–40 years on, your original purchase could yield into a prudent investment. Don't laugh. But if 30 years ago you had purchased tins of Dunhill-made 965 (as opposed to Dunhill-branded), Standard Mixture, Royal Yacht, etc., the returns would have been staggering. Now, please, don't go out and start investing good money on tobacco like you may have done with your briars. Your money will be much safer and weather the long haul best in the equity and debt markets. Just think of your ever burgeoning tobacco larder as your little hedge against an uncertain future.

Security and storage are other matters to carefully evaluate. Think rats. Earlier in the book I commented on my chest of tobacco drawers, the "drawers," and how the mice took no interest in the pipe tobacco I had deposited there. I believe this to be true but only so far as the interest of one mouse was insufficiently aroused to poke around. Perhaps he took only snuff and cigars. The other members of his family may have been less fussy.

Living on a farm one must have plenty of healthy cats, and not too well fed so that they are inclined to hunt. They say that living in New York City one is never more than six feet from a rat. I would add that the country squire is no different than his cousin, the city dude, and he will find an abundance of rodents in the fields, in and about older farm buildings, especially in close proximity to a stream.

Rodents chew and gnaw for a living. Don't think for a minute that they will be unable to smell your precious tobacco because it is sealed in plastic within a heavy carton. They will. And they will chew threw anything to get at it, including timber, fiberglass, screening, and plaster. They may not feast on it as you would, but they will leave their mark, forever tainting its delectable smoking qualities.

To security or the risk of theft, I think there's a possibility, but in general, it is unlikely because the modern-day thief is looking for goods of liquidity to easily fence. Besides, the younger crook would be educated in the dangers of smoking and would probably not choose such reckless behavior as smoking, and to that of the pipe, inconceivable!

20

Truths, Half-Truths and Lies

*To kill an error is as good a service as, and sometimes even better
than, the establishing of a new truth or fact.*

—Charles Darwin

What is it about men? Some will accept anything they are told, while others will question everything. The agreeable type often makes for a good companion. The disagreeable type is challenging, makes for a quarrelsome relationship, but oftentimes offers a great ride through life. This chapter is filled with truths (at least to me until disproved), half-truths (could go either way), and lies (flat-out fiction, but sans malice).

Pipe smoking has a long and rich history. Like any history, time has a way of fashioning it to suit particular needs. There's no arguing about much of the physical world, at least not if you understand chemistry and physics. Few of us have such a scientific background, and so we must plug along through life trying to make heads or tails of things. As pipemen, we do know how to effect a perfect combustion in our little bowls of wood. That would be enough for the dullard, but I know the real pipeman is inquisitive, and while he may be agreeable with matters demanding his circumspection, he will question that which he knows differently through his own familiarity.

Here, then, is a good heaping of pipe theories, some tired and hanging on to the culture and some *au courant*, all trailing around in conversations as far ranging as Web-based digital diaries, or blogs, to formal gatherings of men at their clubs. Most would agree these are self-evident, the beliefs having been bandied around for our entire smoking lives. I delve deep to highlight fact from fallacy. The *truths* are marked "="; *half-truths* "±"; and *lies* "≠."

Cool pipes

Sandblasted pipes smoke cooler (≠) Such a pipe may indeed have 10–100 percent more surface area than one with a smooth surface, but if your bowl is properly filled, most of the heat from combustion will exit vertically not horizontally. In briars that are over-filled and tamped, or where there is a tamped lid of ash that causes a dampening affect on the draft, the heat will begin to transfer to the wood. The radiating heat will be cooled more quickly against a larger surface, but not enough to make a smoker notice any perceptible difference, because a typical sandblasted or rusticated surface is far from a true radiator design—like one that's air- or liquid-cooled with integral radiating fins, like the Porsche pipe. Pack your pipe correctly with the right kind of tobacco and you'll achieve similar results in a pipe with whatever type finish you desire.

Thick-walled pipes smoke cooler (≠) Beyond some visually obvious point, a pipe bowl's wall that is too thick merely adds weight. Anyway, as in the previous citation, because heat rises and because most of a pipe's heat is not transferred to the wood but goes up the "chimney," there's no need for all that wood, except for those who like the look and prefer the heft in their smokeables.

Long pipes smoke cooler (≠) With this untruth I have assembled the triumvirate of hot air on coolness. While it is true that in a well-stoked pipe much of the fire goes up the flue, the vacuum created by puffing will pull some of it through the shank and into the mouth. I suppose if the pipe's shank is several meters long, heat will be absorbed by the wood. But your average long-shanked pipe, like a Canadian or lumberman, has typically three to five inches of shank, and given the velocity with which smoke travels on a "drag," there's not enough time for any cooling to take place. Some say that these long, mostly wood-shanked pipes smoke cooler because briar has a greater specific heat number than vulcanite. This may be true, but my empirical observations find no noticeable difference.

Hot tobacco and ethereal smoke

Burley bites (±) All tobacco bites (i.e., can cause discomfort to the mouth by over-sensitizing the lining). It just depends on what you're doing with it. Burley is best left for "chaw," but is used everywhere in the production of aromatic mixtures—invariably, it will bite and burn—and in English mixtures.

Full-bodied mixtures weigh heavy on the constitution (±) Actually, the opposite holds true. Balkan, English, and Scottish mixtures, with their requisite latakia component, are low in nicotine, and it is the nicotine that's the drug. Nevertheless, those English mixtures with high latakia percentages—especially those that are pressed—can bring you to lightheadedness.

Tobacco can be rehumidified (±) The jury is not back on this one. Moisture can be returned to tobacco, though it ain't easy to get the amount just so. The trick is whether or not it will behave like the good stuff you know it to be. Some postulate that part of the destruction of drying is that the essential oils may have been carried off with the original moisture. Exactly what the essential oils are nobody has ever told me, and I'm starting to get peeved because I think those same people who cite the oils don't know either.

The best tobacco mixtures are made in the United States (=) I have only to ask my pipe and it tells me so.

Mixtures get better with age (±) Be careful: some will, but most won't. Go back to chapter 10 for the skinny.

Real pipemen smoke the entire bowl of tobacco (±) Much like the cigarette or cigar, the last bit of tobacco from a pipe (especially when smoking aromatics) is charged with nicotine, and oftentimes, is rank. If the taste begins going south, no shame, dump the bowl out and start over.

Add a small piece of fruit to your pouch to keep the 'baccy fresh (=) One square-inch of lemon or lime peel is more than enough to keep the humidity of your tobacco in your pouch just right for several days. It will not turn moldy.

I began the writing of this book only one time but discovered I kept coming back repeatedly to end it. While you have a goodly number of pages ahead of you still to read, I was blessed with the following contribution from a fine friend that captures a dimension of pipe smoking few have articulated. I decided to place it here—it would be fitting on any page—the last, perfect, superlative morsel, which I decided to add to the book thereby ending my labor. The words, I feel, are the truest so far, but you decide: truth, half-truth, or lie?

It is the smoke, not the taste from tobacco, which explains why the pipeman is so rapt by his pipe ( ) "The perfection of the tobacco … is certainly necessary to the pleasure of smoking; but it isn't the most important thing, for the pleasure that good tobacco gives is only sensual.… So listen. The principal pleasure of smoking consists in the sight of the smoke. You must never see it leaving the pipe, but only from the corner of your mouth, at exact intervals, never too often. So true is it that this is the principal pleasure, you will never see a blind man who enjoys smoking" (Giacomo Casanova, *The Story of My Life*, Penguin Classic, 2001, 121).

The cut of a pipe

The orifice design makes a difference (±) Design-obsessed collectors and pipemen will fuss endlessly over the "finish" of the bit, or lip, on a pipe and its orifice. I'm not speaking about the diameter of the pipe's draft bore but of the exit point at the mouth-end of the pipe. Without getting into fluid dynamics—I spent seven years of my life practicing as a field sales engineer—I will say that as it relates to turbulence (which some feel is important to the smoke entering one's mouth), as long as the orifice has at least the same area of the bore with no changes in direction or other obstruction, the stream of smoke will enter the mouth equally well in the sense of concentration and be dissipated to fill the volume of the mouth. Whether the orifice is painstakingly smoothed and opened through hours of crafting by the pipesmith, or is left square-cut, as is the practice with injection-molded mouthpieces, it has no affect on a pipe causing a hot-spot in the mouth. But I have decided to give partial marks for style, because a well-cut bit is and should be appreciated by the pipeman as much as he gives credit to the rest of a well-fashioned briar. With that said, the twin-bore mouthpiece is nothing more than propaganda and is not worth the extra cleaning it entails.

Bent pipes gurgle (=) Save the lordly calabash, most half- to fully-bent pipes trap moisture, unable to rise to the occasion. Have your cleaners handy to avoid being a nuisance to those within earshot.

Pits are flaws; fills are pernicious (≠) Much ink has been dispensed and vitriol penned in the pages of Pipedom's hobby press on the debate concerning fills and flaws. There should be little to argue about in pipes and tobacco, so those who care too much and with little else to do—including this author—have weighed in on why it matters. Simply stated, a tiny sand-pit on the surface of an otherwise smooth-surface briar, is no more a flaw than a mole or wart on the face of a typical pipeman. And while a fill is just a little cosmetics to cover up what some feel should not be paraded around in public, a cover-up can become an ugly matter if a pipesmith lies about its concealment. All the same, depending on his market, it may or may not be good business for him to announce his production techniques. Under full disclosure, neither fill nor flaw will keep you *out* of the club.

The pipe is a phallic symbol (=) Isn't everything?

The greatest pipe ever made: the Dunhill Shell Briar (=) No debate here. Closing in on 100 years, this storied pipe design is the mother of the most copied format in Pipedom.

Oil-cured pipes have a nut-like taste when smoked (≠) The first smoke or two, okay, I have noticed something, but I will assign no part marks. Pure mercantilism here. The purpose for the oil infusion is not to alter the taste but to rid the wood of lingering, bitter-tasting tannins.

Bowl coatings prevent burnout and build a more uniform cake (±) A quality pipe, with a caring and patient smoker behind it, will not burn itself before a natural cake forms. Regardless, the mysterious coating—carbon, crushed nutshells, water glass (sodium silicate), or otherwise—is nothing more than a value-added feature worthy of marketing hype to a naive public. As for the rapid puffer, it is he who the pipesmith is most concerned with.

More bore draft is better than less (=) You need sufficient draft for the combustion to go on, with or without you. Pipes snuff themselves out because they're packed too tight and because of restricted draft through the airway. In the past, too many factory pipes were undersized in this regard. Today, artisan pipesmiths know better. Just the same, don't run around looking for someone to drill-out your pipes for a wider bore believing they'll smoke better because it was written about by an über collector and now trendy. Evaluate each pipe on its own merits. Pipes that whistle like a tea kettle clearly need attention: there's an obstruction and it must be removed. Upon careful circumspection you might find that the source of your smoking woes is not the pipe but you. Adopt the edict of less is more as it pertains to the filling of your pipe. There was a time when I was guilty of overfilling, packing as much tobacco as I could for the longest smoke possible; a counterproductive move. If one of one's goals in smoking is to taste and smell the tobacco, airflow must be unrestricted. But this is only the beginning! Be attentive to your habits of tamping the embers. Be attentive to the build-up of ash. If the hardest thing in smoking a pipe is filling it, then the second hardest thing is maintaining the correct pack to the bowl. A gentle hand will solve the problem pipe long before a drill bit should ever be a consideration.

Acrylic bits are not as comfortable as those of vulcanite (±) Generally, I would agree that, millimeter for millimeter, vulcanite is easier on the teeth. But where I acquiesce is when the pipesmith puts the time into hand-cutting the lip thin enough such that the acrylic bit does closely approach the comfort of rubber. (Castello of Cantu, Italy, proves the point, using acrylic ... exclusively.)

Meerschaums are fun to smoke and watch while they change color (≠) Nothing could be further from the truth. Far and away the hardest thing in Smokedom to accomplish is curing a beautiful color transformation to a finely-carved meerschaum. They don't color uniformly, even with the plethora of olden- and modern-day prescriptions at the pipeman's disposal with which to experiment. The pursuit is noble but, alas, quite often futile.

Little pipes don't weigh much (=) Did you ever catch someone next to you lift a small, thin-walled pipe and comment on its weightlessness? Well, if the pipe is only five inches long there's not a whole lot that can be there. True, some pipes do possess perhaps more heft than they should, but a classic-shaped pipe of, say, a group 3 size, will weigh 25–30 grams. So stop being surprised!

Pipe style and worth

Straight pipemen smoke their pipe on the left side of their mouth (≠) There was a time when the side of your mouth in which you clenched your pipe determined the type of tobacco smoker you were. The left side indicated a preference for English and Virginia mixtures; the right side, aromatics. If you smoked in the middle, you liked going both ways, or, in the argot of the 70s and 80s, you were *bi*. Not. For whatever it's worth, by casual observance, more pipemen have chosen the left side.

Men prefer straights; women prefer bents (=) "When females go to the store to buy a pipe for their boyfriends, they always buy a curved pipe. When the male goes, he buys a straight pipe, but a curved pipe reminds women of a kindly old professor, the old philosopher, old granddad, solidarity, understanding, that kind of thing" (John G. Koeltl and John S. Kiernan, editors, *The Litigation Manual* [Chicago: American Bar Association, 1999],

103). If quoted in any other type of book, this could be misconstrued as a sexual reference. In the context of this book, however, I am unabashed in stating my preference for straights! And I believe, at least historically, straight briars have outsold bents at least two to one. If Koeltl and Kiernan are correct, this could be construed as just another example of that classic metaphor for the differences between the sexes, men are from Mars, women are from Venus.

Pipe smoking is good for you (=) Could anything be more self-evident to the pipeman? Now, all that's left for us is to tell the story to the anti-smoking heretics.

Pipemen think like a sage and act like a Samaritan (±) This is nothing more than a self-fulfilling prophesy, but that's okay. If a small apparatus like a pipe can make you truly better, then I'm all for it. Perhaps, after smoking one for at least 20 years you'll have something to show for it.

A pipe renaissance is underway (≠) Poppycock! Renaissance is a powerful word and a far-reaching phenomenon. When pipe shows even one-tenth the scope of a Chicagoland begin popping up in every region of the country, then should you believe it!

Slow smoking is good for you (=) Most of the time, smoking is a solitary pursuit. Unusual is it to see more than two pipemen together enjoying each other's mutual interest in the pastime. Larger gatherings are typically well secluded at smoking clubs and pipe shows. For those with a competitive streak, there are competitions where men and women gather to see who can smoke three grams of tobacco from identical pipes the longest without relighting. An insufferably slow sport, the challenge drags on as the pipe of one smoker after another goes out. It has its moments of jocularity, but the fellows are typically quite serious, as the prizes can be meaningful, like a new pipe or tins of tobacco, and the chance to have your name engraved on a swell trophy cup. For some reason, Europeans take such events more seriously than their Yankee cousins, often wearing team colors and indigenous costumes. Nevertheless, American pipemen can boast of their own national association, UPCA, or the United Pipe Clubs of America, that promotes clubs and slow-smoke contests. I encourage you to join in, smoke a pinch of tobacco everyone seems to complain about, and test your skills at a one-matcher against your best pipe-smoking friends. It's really off-beat and too much fun.

Pipemen need extra pockets (=) In addition to life's body clutter, such as a cellphone, keychain, wallet, coins, money-clip, pocket-knife, and rabbit's-foot (whose foot is it anyway?), he must have the carrying capacity for a pipe and pouch, matches or lighter, cleaners and pipe-tool. I have found that a tweed jacket works well. So does a vest, such as those worn by land surveyors, fishermen, and men who for no particular reason like wearing one and look good in them. If you're not attending a pipe-smoker's event, make an effort to leave the club and travel pins at home rather than affixing them to your clothing, or you'll look too much the part of a scoutmaster.

You require the velocity of a buffing wheel to rejuvenate your briar (±) I have no hands-on experience with a buffer, but I have heard both for and against its use to clean and polish a tired pipe. In the hands of anyone but a professional pipe refinisher, a pipe put to a high-speed (1750 rpm) wheel will be ruined.

A pipe should rest upright in the rack (≠) Long ago, the debate raged on as to whether the pipe was to be put to rest bowl down or bowl up in the rack. Before effective pipe cleaners made the scene, it made more sense to have the bowl orientated in the downward position so that moisture could run down the shank and be absorbed by the cake. It's no longer an issue, so I encourage you to make your own choice based on the design of your pipe racks.

EBay prices are representative of actual/fair-market value (=) Does this mean that the unsmoked 1956 Dunhill Whangee shell briar churchwarden I purchased a few years ago for $100 on eBay one early Monday morning (1:15 a.m.!), just 30 minutes after it was listed as "Buy It Now" was a really great snag, a steal, a price well below current and general market values? Yes! If this hard-to-find, stunning pipe were listed as the norm, a seven-day auction, it might have easily fetched upwards of $1,200, leaving those knowledgeable and practiced collectors battling for it in the remaining seconds before time ran out and the auction closed. Conversely, pipe-collecting newbies with more currency than common sense might have created a different digital-bidding fray, and the price could have far exceeded $1,200! Could my pipe, then, not only be worth $1,200 or, perhaps, an even higher unknown, but likely, price? Yes, under both circumstances.

Why? For all the first-rate and peculiar items listed on eBay, there is the age-old mechanism of supply and demand. The paradigm example for a perfect market where highly liquid stuff trades, is the NYSE or any other long-established and massive-volume equity, debt, or commodities exchange. These are marketplaces where known articles are up for grabs, where supply and demand dictate economic worth at one historical moment in time. As a digital exchange, eBay does not approximate such markets. As an online, merchandise-listing service, or timed auction, as some prefer to call it, eBay is still a relatively nascent marketplace, and those one-off and peculiar bits and pieces, such as tobacciana, do not always attract sufficient market demand—even with the 24/7 access—to determine what some may feel reflects their opinion of true value, but not necessarily market value.

Nevertheless, it is what it is, a representation of market value at one moment in time, regardless of what the articulate seller of pipes feels is fair. The fact that many items regularly go unsold or fail to meet their reserve is proof that much of tobacciana has limited appeal in today's anti-tobacco clime. But this we already know. Even more reason to express caution when valuing a collection. Chances are some items may be difficult to sell quickly or at a profit. Values change with regularity, often unpredictably, like the weather, and eBay's trading mechanism is no different than the other more traditional markets: prices rise and prices fall based on supply and demand and, as my late-evening purchase proved, at odd hours of the day as well. (Proves the old adage that timing is everything, and it also helps to be an occasional insomniac.)

But is market value the same as actual value? If the emotional ties to an object are discounted, then yes, market and actual values are about equal. Clearly, no one, least of all prospective buyers, place a value on sentimentality or goodwill. And as relatively illiquid as most tobacciana stuff is, market value will always be the best judge of actual, fair, replacement, or however you need to define worth. That eBay is not a classic bricks and mortar auction house—there's no hammer to fall when bidding ends—makes it no less an auction. It would not be an untrue statement to say that even the most renowned auction houses have sales that fall short of expectation because of slack demand, disinterest, or economic malaise. But this does not mean that lower realized prices are any less indicative of "current market," albeit to the chagrin of the house and consignor. Alas, in the end, all that one can assuredly take to the bank is that no economic axiom exists to better explain inherent value than the law of supply and demand.

You are the last pipeman (=) Look around and see for yourself.

21

What Others Have Said

People of mediocre ability sometimes achieve outstanding success because they don't know when to quit. Most men succeed because they are determined to.

—George Allen, Sr.

WITH more than the usual volume of feedback I received with the release of the first edition of *Confessions*, it was clear to me that pipemen of all persuasions—those who agreed with many of my declarations and those who did not—were curious as to what my take would be on a variety of topics salient to the pipeman. From $1,000 pipes to tweed; from pipe shows to the burgeoning class of hobby pipe carvers; from what English and Balkan mixtures I smoke day in day out to blended Scotches versus single malts; and so on. Whether at the club, pipe shows, the office, or online, I am approached as an expert on such varied topics because I have written a few books, published many others, on a very narrow topic which many pipemen have a keen interest in. While all of this recent attention was not wholly unexpected and is a result of my own doing, I do not avoid it because I like to be seen as helpful. Helping is a rather good investment because most of us are in need of aid on a regular basis. And knowing that you can only reap what you sow, the more grants of altruism the greater the chances help will be there when you need it.

There are those who are able to react spontaneously to situations and to verbalize their sentiments in carefully constructed and witty dialogue. I am not one of those, and I believe it is the rare person with the innate ability to express himself well *in* the moment. I do much better articulating my opinion, ink on paper, after a good night of rest and reflection.

Charles Scribner, Jr., the last generation of the great New York publishing dynasty, once said, "Reading is a means of thinking with another person's mind; it forces you to stretch your own." With the purchase of this book you committed yourself to seeing things from my point of view. Whether any of it has given you pause to reflect will, I suppose, means that you have reaped some personal benefit. But I'm just one man with limited thought, scribbling away to a culture of pipemen, some seasoned, others very much still engaged, who wish to reaffirm their dedication to a lifestyle focused, in part, on that which many smart people among us who feel smoking tobacco—even in a pipe—is counterproductive to cleanliness, good health, and to preserving an upright moral foundation.

So, let's broaden our focus on who we pipemen are. To do so, you will need to, like Charles Scribner, Jr. said, stretch your own mind. However, as in this Rorschach-like literary review, do so abstractly.

What follows is a list of quotations divided by topic and in no particular order. Read each quotation, and then pause to reflect on what it means to you as a pipeman. And, if you *take* to one or two, memorize them, and you'll be primed to dispense pithy repartee like no one else and as if on cue.

Hope ... "What we hope ever to do with ease, we must learn first to do with diligence."   —Samuel Johnson

Health ... "The only way to keep your health is to eat what you don't want, drink what you don't like, and do what you'd rather not."   —Mark Twain

Talent ... "I have no special talent. I am only passionately curious."
                                    —Albert Einstein

Self-Confidence ... "The way to develop self-confidence is to do the thing you fear and get a record of successful experiences behind you."
                                    —William Jennings Bryan

Courage ... "Courage is rightly esteemed the first of human qualities ... because it is the quality which guarantees all others."   —Winston Churchill

Conviction ... "I have brought myself, by long meditation, to the conviction that a human being with a settled purpose must accomplish it, and that nothing can resist a will which will stake even existence upon its fulfillment."
                                    —Benjamin Disraeli

Youth ... "Youth has no age."   —Pablo Picasso

Civility ... "The civility which money will purchase is rarely extended to those who have none."   —Charles Dickens

Style ... "One man's style must not be the rule of another's."   —Jane Austen

Quality ... "Quality is decided by the depth at which the work incorporates the alternatives within itself, and so masters them."   —Theodor Adorno

Taste ... "He is not to pass for a man of reason who stumbles upon reason by chance but he who knows it and can judge it and has a true taste for it."
—Francois de La Rochefoucauld

Government ... "That government is best which governs least."
—Henry David Thoreau

Scotch ... "For her fifth wedding, the bride wore black and carried a scotch and soda."   —Phyllis Battelle

Smoking 1 ... "I know a man who gave up smoking, drinking, sex, and rich food. He was healthy right up to the day he killed himself."   —Johnny Carson

Smoking 2 ... "It is now proved beyond doubt that smoking is one of the leading causes of statistics."   —Fletcher Knebel

Smoking 3 ... "Smoking calms me down. It's enjoyable. I don't want politicians deciding what is exciting in my life."   —David Hockney

Smoking 4 ... "Taking in and blowing out smoke? And now you see girls smoking cigars. It got to be such a fad. Girls on the covers of magazines, smoking cigars. Give me a break. I didn't want to be a part of that. I don't like 'popular'."   —James Coburn

22

You Might be a Pipeman if ...

Thank you, God, for this good life and forgive us if we do not love it enough.

—Garrison Keillor

WHO among us, city slicker and country bumpkin alike, has not seen or heard comedian Jeff Foxworthy's droll Americana humor poking fun at our more rural citizenry? "You might be a redneck if you think Taco Bell is the Mexican phone company." Perhaps, "You might be a redneck if "you think a woman who bowls 'out of your league' bowls on a different night." Or how about, "You might be a redneck if you think the last words to *The Star-Spangled Banner* are 'Gentlemen, start your engines'."

In the same vain, one can study people from all walks of life and find their mannerisms and lifestyles unique, peculiar, and funny. And so it must be for the pipe smoker, be he one new to the cadre or, indeed, a veritable pipeman. Here, then, is an assemblage of observations—in no particular order—of things distinctive, funny, strange, and true of the man who smokes tobacco in a pipe.

(Thank you to Kevin Kaplan of the Seattle Pipe Club for the inspiration to write this piece.)

You might be a pipeman if ...

❖ You give serious consideration when your wife demands you make a choice between her and your habit of smoking a pipe.

❖ You think there are worse things in life than preferring to smoke Cavendish tobaccos.

❖ The word budget never comes to mind when you fall in love with a pipe you have to have.

❖ Teenagers think you're cool because you could be smoking pot in that pipe.

❖ You consider incinerating your smoke-saturated clothes before greeting your wife after a night at the pipe club.

❖ You daydream of your next "pipe."

❖ You lead your wife to believe a pipe cannot cost more than $25.

❖ You dissuade your wife from accompanying you to a pipe show.

❖ You take great pride in seeing a stranger smoking a pipe.

❖ You think your latest mixture discovery cannot possibly be outdone.

❖ Finally, you have a good explanation for carrying a man-bag.

❖ You find the idea of being unable to smoke in a public elevator undemocratic.

❖ You abscond with your child's pre-school project pipe cleaners because you're fresh out in the study.

❖ Your tobaccos dry out faster than you can smoke them only to realize that many are better that way.

❖ You think nothing of taking puffs from your briar in between breaths from your oxygen cylinder.

❖ Time intervals are measured by the time it takes to smoke a "bowl."

❖ When going on a trip, you put more consideration into your smoking kit than your valise of clothes.

❖ You feel like a blessed child without a care in the world when you are at a pipe show, surrounded by friends—every man with a pipe.

❖ You shipwreck on a deserted island and you had given due forethought to the possibility and packed your smokeables accordingly. Unfortunately, they went down with the ship!

❖ You place the comfort of others above yourself and suffer "smokeless" until the opportunity presents itself.

❖ You contemplate such opportunities as what it must have been like to light up a dress pipe during intermission at the theatre or opera.

❖ You own a deerstalker cap.

❖ You installed a pipe rack on the dashboard of your car.

❖ You cease to be happy with your favorite tobacco because, well, just because!

❖ You just feel the world would right itself of its problems if more men smoked the briar.

❖ If you've ever caught yourself asking, "Honey, have you seen my pipe?" (*Courtesy* Kevin Kaplan)

❖ You ask your wife if smoking a magnum bull dog makes you look fat. (*Courtesy* Kevin Kaplan)

❖ You long for the moor but have never left the city.

❖ Gerald Ford has become your favorite president because he used to smoke a pipe. What a relief Nixon never indulged in one.

❖ You once thought tobacco couldn't get any better than Borkum Riff Cherry Cavendish.

❖ You once gave consideration to wearing a belt holster to hold your pipe.

❖ You realize—oh the embarrassment!—that you may be the first to go *out* in a slow-smoke pipe competition.

❖ You have given momentary consideration to the effects of smoking on your carbon footprint and have decided you can live with the "fallout."

❖ You are a solitary soul and have no need for the companionship of other pipemen to get on with pure smoking pleasure.

❖ You are gregarious, personable, and enjoy the company of other pipemen and so relish your local pipe-club's monthly meeting.

❖ Saving the best for last, I recount this anecdote told to me by a young, burgeoning pipeman who had read the first edition of *Confessions*, I shall refer to him as S.T.: "My employer is a health nut and an avid anti-smoking campaigner. He offered health screenings at the studio and as an incentive to participate, he gave those who did a $100 Amex gift card. I went to the health screening, got a clean bill of health and used the gift card to buy a pipe."

You might be a pipe collector if ...

❖ You never give up the hope of finding a $5 Dunhill at an antique mall. And if ever faced with such a find, feel compelled to ask for the customary 10 percent discount!

❖ You confess that your best smokers happen not to be your most expensive acquisitions.

❖ In your divorce your wife got your pipe collection, you got the house, and you felt outdone. (*Courtesy* Kevin Kaplan)

❖ You've considered how your wife will dispose of your collection upon your demise.

❖ Giving back to the hobby means more to you than purchasing the next piece of wood you cannot live without.

❖ You collect French pipes, but I think not. How strange. The birthplace of the briar, yet to hear of anyone with an affinity for the bruyère so manufactured, I have not. The English popularized the pipe, and more men collect English-made pipes than any other.

❖ You have two pipes. But really, isn't true collecting so much more of a pursuit than simply sheer accumulation of the article?

❖ You're fascinated by pipe nomenclature and disappointed when some no-account has buffed it off of a perfectly good discovery you've made.

❖ In your search of the "Holy Grail" for what you have specialized in, you have finally come to grasp the truth that a collection can never be complete, that the journey, every difficult and sometimes dear step of it, is why you do it. In the end, the collector is much more than the sum of his collection.

❖ You think your pipes are rare, beyond compare.

❖ You know the last year Dunhill applied the patent stamp to its pipes, yet are unable to remember the grandkids' birthdays.
❖ You cancel your *Playboy* subscription and sign up for *Pipes & Tobaccos* or the North American Society of Pipe Collectors' *The Pipe Collector*.

And you might be a pipeman if ... in spite of it all, you continue, undeterred, with a lifestyle you can call your own. Light up, man, you deserve it!

23

What if You Should Die?

If you want to make God laugh, tell him about your plans.
—Woody Allen

WHEN you die your pipes will join you in the ground. I know this to be true not from direct, personal experience but from being a keen observer of the demise of others. On one occasion, I did not interrupt the event because I knew the man and his pipes. Both were better off in the ground, whence they came. With the other corpse, it was a wholly different affair. I was late on the scene and the place had turned quite malodorous; from the pipes, not the stiff. I admired the man as much as I did his pipes, and he had some fine ones. But the widow, in haste, and who could have known better, was bent on a new beginning and it was to be one without Latakia.

So what about your pipes? Have you given thought to their care when you will be no longer upon the earth but beneath it? We've all heard of the living will, when you're in some sort of vegetative state, on life support, with a shelf life of that of a melon, and no longer in a state of mind to make those key decisions, such as billiard or bulldog, English or Virginia. For every veritable pipeman has the responsibility of preparing his estate for this eventuality. Consideration for the wife and children are done with dispatch. Your average attorney will know what to do here. But your collection deserves your very careful attention and must not be relegated to someone indifferent and who may very well harbor a distaste for smoking and all of its appurtenances, including you, Mr. Dead.

There is no reason to be melancholy about the process. In fact, careful thought about who should get what can be a pleasurable time spent. And there will be no better and heartfelt way to show your affection to the beneficiary of your kindness than by bequeathing a pipe to that chosen friend who cherished and coveted it almost as much as you did when you were still around to enjoy it in their good company. The value of such a gift is immeasurable and will be a treasure that has succeeded in attaining a second coming by its new owner.

But not all pipes should be so well treated. Many will be well past their prime, tired beyond good repair, and deserve a well-earned rest, and thus, suitable interment.

I would like to believe that most pipes that have reached this staging point would have been given and received such understanding and consideration, but, alas, once beyond the reach of its master, anything is possible. And so pipes are discarded as so much bath water or kitchen waste. And whose fault is that?

Life is messy, whether your means are meager or substantial. Now is the time to come clean with your wife or family and to fess up to what you've done: you've spent some serious dollars piecing together your pipe collection (all of those $25 purchases have added up, haven't they?). That regardless of the degree of indifference those close to you may have towards your existence, they need to know that their show of affection will not have been wasted. They will be rewarded with a pipe! I suppose it would be a cruel joke if that's all that one would end up getting at the reading of your last will and testament, especially if they didn't smoke, hated your smoke, or wanted the camp by the lake instead; but then again, maybe not if the relation was one particularly worthwhile of your affection. Because a pipe is not always a pipe. But the camp by the lake *with* the pipe would be better.

I have often wondered why some brands of estate pipes have outlasted their lesser-known cousins. Ounce per ounce, the old Dunhills have faired better than any others. True, they have been around longer than most other brands; their presence quickly spread inter-continental; but I think the defining reason for their longevity is because the brand was always considered a luxury good as opposed to a commodity, and a practical one at that. Dunhill may be known more for fashion than pipes for the last 30 or 40 years, yet it will be the women folk who recognize the value in the piece because it is a Dunhill and because it was made in England. So the Dunhills will be saved from the garbage chute. The same has not and will not happen with the brands unbeknownst to the executor of the estate.

Mind you, of the last 15 years, the Internet has offered up a great outlet for the true estate pipe, eBay. These orphans will get a second chance. And if there's any life left in them, they will eventually end up in the hands of yet another pipeman who will put them to proper use.

Even those run-of-the-mill, over-smoked Dunhill Bruyères that really should be chucked, have been saved, many lovingly restored, all because someone—not a pipeman—knew that a Dunhill product, whatever it was, was a cut above the rest and deserved reprieve. There are many other pipe brands equally as worthy, but they came from factories that made only pipes, brands that were not diversified in other non-smoking goods, so only the pipemen knew of them. Pity.

Even still, your wishes would be better met by conducting the dispersal of your estate before you die. Do you really need the pipes you no longer smoke or which you haven't unpacked since your last move? You can't take it with you, so sell it now, or gift it to someone who will appreciate it as much as you once did.

Charitable giving is a noble deed, but the recipient is often a faceless institution—organized under the 501(c)(3) statute—that will thank you no more than with a slip of paper for you to surrender to your accountant for the preparation of your 1040. The act of gifting a cherished item from your collection will yield no tax deduction, but it can be done any day of the year and will put you face-to-face with the recipient for you to experience their surprise and joy at your unexpected largesse. I think that when you experience the returns from both such acts of generosity, you will learn that "giving it away," in person, ought to become part of your overall portfolio of life.

Like me, you're an incomparable to the likes of the archetype philanthropist, Andrew Carnegie, or his modern-day facsimile, Bill Gates, nevertheless the decisions you make about your collection and its dispersal can have a profound and far-reaching effect. The act of giving is infectious. I firmly believe that most of us who have received another's generosity, whether or not in time of need, will endeavor to reciprocate such altruism in their own way. And so, the original gesture has multiplied in number and value exponentially. That pipe so admired by an acquaintance, one time the best face of your collection, is the embodiment of an opportunity to enrich the life of another. Lo and behold, the truism that it is better to give than receive has reaffirmed itself once again.

And I think the most value from such transactions of goodwill occur when the recipient at first glance appears to be wholly undeserving. That person, yes, even that pipeman!—and we all have a short list of them—that needs a refresher in how to be a good, kind soul, will be stunned when you recognize him with, say, a vintage tin of My Mixture 965 or a briar of a shape you know this man collects. You have the power to turn him around, transforming him into a superior pipeman.

Significant collections deserve special mention here. Those collectors of prominence who have assembled world-class or museum-grade collections have similar decisions to make and greater opportunities to consider. You think your briars are precious? You ain't seen nothing! There are collectors, mostly in Europe, who spend not hundreds but thousands and sometimes tens of thousands of dollars on single pipes and whole collections. And they have purchased only the finest pieces that have come their way, always refining their pursuit and thus acquisitions. They're the stuff, literally, that museums are made of. Usually, they are centered around meerschaums, less often briars. Individuals of this rarified breed have struggled their entire adult existence to assemble something that would define what a world-class pipe collection is. Sadly, as confessed much earlier in the book, the cultural museums that such collectors could have relied upon to take their collection for safekeeping and public viewing (and just a little bit of eternal remembrance), are now mostly shuddered. It's regrettable, too, because in all likelihood the collection will be sold at auction to the highest bidder(s), forever being split apart into all of its pieces. On the other hand, one can maintain that the overall benefit from the scattering of the collection will yield far greater benefits for all of its new owners.

I suppose there are museums that still absorb such tobacciana, but these days chances run high the pipes etc. will be packed away into its bowels never to resurface until the museum itself is in need of new space and decides to auction some of its "dead wood," or ironically, closes its doors once and for all.

For such collections, it is the well-established auction house where the collection must be taken. For meerschaums, Europe is the best option. With briars, smoked or unsmoked, your best avenue is to either approach one of the many U.S.-based Internet sellers—the modern-day tobacconists— specializing in choice, high-grade stuff, or by selling it through an experienced e-merchant at the best online auction house that is not an auction in the true sense of the term, eBay. If your collection is substantial and the best of the best, take it to a pro, he'll have the money to buy it spot, thereby saving you the aggravation of the usual liquidity issue of things like old smoking pipes and related items.

I'm sure you'll never get what you paid for it, so be disappointed now and get over it. You knew in the beginning when you got stung by the collecting bug that you were in it for the fun and nothing else. If you get half of what you paid for the stuff when it was acquired, however long ago, consider the money well spent.

24

Mentoring

Laws control the lesser man. Right conduct controls the greater one.

—Mark Twain

TO perpetuate the breed of the quintessential pipe smoker, every pipeman has a duty to tutor the novice and edify the inquisitive. As men, we shall never be for lack of requiring lessons on matters of unique circumstance or for life-changing direction. Frequently, we are standing alone grasping at what to do while at other times, magically, a person is close by with instruction to bring us along. At some point, every budding pipeman was there alone with a pipe, tobacco, and a match and knew not what exactly to do and where that first pipe would take him. "Smoking a pipe is an art. Many years later I bought five fine briar pipes and two or three cheap ones, and took up pipe smoking. I had tampers, scrapers, special lighters, pouches, pipe stands, and other items too numerous to list. Wilse just had one pipe and a can of Prince Albert. I often wished I had paid more attention to Wilse when he explained pipe smoking. After about a year, I decided smoking a pipe properly required an assistant. I had no assistant, so I quit" (James L. Winfree, *I Killed a Bluebird* [Bloomington: www.iuniverse.com, Author's Choice Press, 2003], 42). Had he been under the tutelage of a pipeman, like Wilse, from the start, things would have definitely gone better; but even that first unsavory episode might have become a cherished memory with the passing of time.

The thing is, how many more pipemen would be around today had their initial pipes been enjoyable, savory smokes? Or, how many pipe smokers would continue using the wrong pipe or smoke the mediocre tobacco thinking they were enjoying their smoking affair to its fullest if they were not corrected mid-stream? I wonder. Who am I, you may say to yourself, to supplant my tastes on those of another? I've been accused of arrogance before, but only the timid would scoff at such a proposition. See, people do things the wrong way all the time. It doesn't matter how long they've been at it, it still don't make it right. Sure, functionally the tobacco burns and the taste is pleasant, but is that all there is to it? Certainly not.

They say there is strength in numbers. If this is true, men of the pipe, you had better watch out. The numbers of pipemen here in the United States and elsewhere about the planet are scant—statistically quantified as "insignificant" and categorized as "other" smokers—and, in my estimation, getting smaller as each tired pipeman pulls his last puff before signing off. Everything in the history of man and beast on planet earth has had its time, and the time of the briar pipe, these previous 150 years, is fast approaching its quiet end. Is the pipe worth saving, worth fighting for? I think so, because more than a good smoke, a pipe is a noble lifestyle.

So what are you going to do about it? Write to your congressman to have smoking laws changed? Good luck. More than a pessimist, I'm a cold, hard realist. Apart from the unlikely event of a celebrity, public figure, or British royal taking up the pipe, the hope of longevity for the pipe lies in each and every common pipeman doing little things to rally round our silent confederation of those beholden to the pipe and tobacco.

This means standing up when no one else will and, one by one, mentoring the misguided, counseling the inquisitive, and judiciously beating down the manic anti-smoking public when the opportunity arises. It means being a good chap and helping the other fellow out. It means repaying the debt of your own upbringing. It means striking up a conversation with those curious about why you do it, when everyone else has shed themselves of their own woebegone habits. Mark Twain had it right so long ago when he wrote, "Nothing so needs changing as other people's vices."

Even so, I worry as much about people helping people as I do about the life expectancy of the pipeman. Look, we all mean well, but assisting another with learning the ropes of something as intimate and strange—by today's standards—as smoking is, well, not easily conceivable. If the best we do with teaching our children about sex is to talk to them about abstinence or the use of contraception, then how will we score when the real tough issues such as pipe smoking presents itself? A life—a pipeman's!—might be hanging in the balance. So I advocate teaching your children well. You do want the best for them, don't you? Then don't leave fate to chance! You mucked-up the sex ed. thing real good. The opportunity before you now is much graver, because if the boy fails on his first attempt to smoke a pipe like his dad or uncle did (and you may be dead by the time he's attempting it, remembering how the old man used to smoke his pipe), not only will you be to blame, but, yet again, another man would be out there, alone, doing his level best, trying to smoke an aromatic tobacco in a bent pipe. And what are the chances he'll see it through like you somehow did?

Postscript

SHOULD you have found this little book to be instructive, then its reading was time well spent. Should you have found my irreverence droll or thought-provoking, then it will have been a sound expenditure, I should think. How about entertaining but forgettable? I can have no malice for such a reader because most good books do no better. If some modicum of this material is used to better oneself to more fully derive pleasure from a pipe and tobacco, and to do it in a way befitting the rich style and history of the pipe, then it will have been worth my time and effort to figure this all out by having to string these words together in some facade of order and value.

It's not real hard to smoke a pipe. We're not all brilliant at it, though. I'd like to think there are not too many pipe-smoking idiots among the coterie. Still, the act of smoking properly is something that only the learned and considerate man can achieve. Being a pipeman, at least to me, is something so much more than a mere knowledge of the mechanics of smoking or collecting tobacciana. I've made an attempt at educing the things that I know have made me the pipeman I am. I believe these are, too, the core values that must be unto every pipeman. Pipe and tobacco smoking are very personal objects of fancy. This I know, and so I must yield to anyone who is at odds with my confessions and who decides to strike off on a journey to become his own type of pipeman.

This is the end of the book but will it soon be the end of the pipe and the pipeman? While use of the pipe has been on the wane since the cigarette took off nearly a 150 years ago, will its use continue in this country until there is just one pipeman left standing? Fifty years from now, will the prototypical pipeman become an exhibit of a cultural museum, sandwiched between an obese-sized family dining on cheeseburgers, fries, and sodas at a fast-food joint, and inner-city, tattooed gang-bangers wearing low-riding, cavernously-baggy jeans showing too much underwear ... or not any?

Not so fast lads. Self-ordained oracles about the trade and hobby of pipes and tobacco claim some sort of renaissance going on in the world of pipe smoking. They allege the signs appear before them and take many forms. One of those forms is the number new pipe carvers here and in the E.U. Another is the great number of new, young pipemen coming through the ranks. There are also the signs of a huge movement forming in Russia, and who knows what super economic expectants like China and India will contribute to this renaissance. Those countries are very big. What I want someone to explain to me is that at this late date why has someone not already discovered briar shrubs and meerschaum deposits? And for all the billions of people, there must be at least a few carvers with the talent of Wolfgang Becker or Jim Cooke.

Don't believe it. There are signs to be sure, but I'll not be so quick as to attribute them to some sort of new-world order of pipemen in this country or one spanning the globe. Wishful thinking at best, at least for now.

What I hope for is that every man who decides to take up the pipe do so with the intent of becoming a better man. The pipe is worth saving. More important, a lifestyle needs rescuing and, more critically, resurrecting. If pipe smoking has any prospect of survival, the way of life and interests of the collector- and hobby-focused pipeman must come out of the closet, so to speak, and into our streets and into magazines of lifestyles—the mainstream, both here and abroad. The cigar did it and continues with renewed popularity—it survived the boom and bust of the 1990s. So too can the pipe. But to do so—and this may be difficult for the old and crusty curmudgeons among today's pipemen—the image of the pipe and the pipe smoker must be recast into something new, fresh, and compelling. The well-worn image of the cardigan-clad, old man sporting a pipe must be retired (with affection and humility), but exit he must. In his place, today's 20- or 30-something man must adopt the pipe with responsible smoking as a reinvented lifestyle. He must become a lightning rod for the new pipeman. The future rests in the young.

This is not unthinkable because the time is here before each and every one of us, and I can only confess to what I know to be bona fide and possible.

Born in Montreal, GBS has long defined his lifestyle by the pipe: sometimes a calabash, on occasion a clay, but mostly a briar. Town, country, and the bush by canoe, his pipe is never far. He lives with his wife and son on a salmon stream on Puget Sound, Washington.

A Pipeman's Library

other titles for your consideration from ...

Briar Books Press

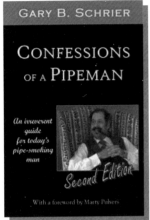

Confessions of a Pipeman ... an irreverent guide for to-day's pipe-smoking man, Second Edition by Gary B. Schrier
Not a how-to book, *Confessions* digs deep to uncover the soul of the pipeman. Defined, analyzed, constructed, and instructed, Schrier lays bare all that the man with his pipe is and who he should be. Critical yet understanding, informative yet opinionated, yet all the while humorous and contemporary. *Confessions* is unlike any other pipe-smoker's book. Get it. Study its lessons, and become a better pipeman, guaranteed. With a foreword by Marty Pulvers. 50% more content than the first edition. $20

The Pipe Smoker's Tobacco Book by Robert F. Winans
A 70's classic, the only tobacco book of its kind written by a tobacco salesman exclusively for the pipe smoker. The central theme is the various tobaccos from their regions around the world, how they differ chemically, and what it means to the pipe smoker who looks for specific attributes from the divers mixture types. A good read. A gem that more pipemen need for their library. This is the original, first-edition book, not a reprint. $12

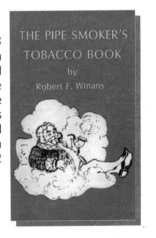

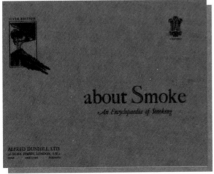

About Smoke ... An Encyclopaedia of Smoking. 5th Edition 1928 by Alfred Dunhill
The ultimate smoker's catalogue from the most famous pipeman's address for over 100 years, Dunhills, 30 Duke Street, St. James's, London. Never again will such a story of merchandise be told as in this 190-page catalogue of pipes, tobacco, cigars, cigarettes, lighters, and smoker's requisites. A masterpiece defining the great age of smoking. Part one of the great pipe-catalogue trilogy. Reprint. $25

www.briarbooks.com

BBB Catalogue No. XX by Adolph Frankau & Co. Ltd.

A most fantastic discovery of the greatest briar-pipe catalogue there ever was: the 1912 wholesale catalogue of the wares of Blumfeld's Best Briars! Imagine, over 450 pages of pipes and smoker's requisites pictured. Breathtaking! Nothing from the period is excluded, including calabashes, clays, and meerschaums. Includes a free color copy of the 1947 Frankau & Co.'s 100-Year celebration booklet telling the story and international presence of the famous BBB brand. You'll think you've died and gone to pipe heaven. Part two of the great pipe-catalogue trilogy. Reprint. $35

BBB 100 Years in the Service of Smokers
by Adolph Frankau & Co. Ltd.

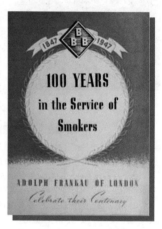

In 1947, the makers of the BBB mark celebrated its centenary with the publication of this 20-page, full-color booklet highlighting the great men of the trade who devoted their lives to establishing the world-wide presence of one of the most renown briars in history. This wonderfully-illustrated reflection gives one the romantic feel the older pipemen of today will remember as the greatest pipe-smoking era in the history of modern man. (Free with an order of the *BBB Catalogue No. XX*.) Reprint. $10

Bo Nordh, Pipemaker by Jan Andersson

This charming story, told by close friend and founder of the Pipe Club of Sweden, Jan Andersson, is sure to please those with a penchant for straight grain and innovative design. A fitting and classy tribute to the late master pipesmith. An all-color, 130-page extravaganza of exquisite shapes, stunning grain, and vignettes of Nordh's friends and collectors of his work. Second printing. $40

The Loewé Pipe Packet by Loewé & Schrier

In its day, a better pipe could not be had, particularly one with such impeccable grain. The most discerning pipemen smoked Loewé. A handsomely assembled packet of the 1910 (92 pp.) and 1926 (24 pp.) catalogues by Loewé of the Haymarket; the 1926 booklet of the firm's reflections on 70 years in the trade; and the Pipeman's Portfolio, a photo display of exquisite early Loewé pipes. Part three of the great pipe-catalogue trilogy. Original and reprint. $40

A Pipeman's Christmastime Companion Set
by Alfred Dunhill & Briar Books Press

A book within a book! Much like the vintage companion sets of two or more briar pipes to a fitted case, we present two hereto before relatively unknown works from Dunhill. The centerpiece, *About Smoke Gifts Edition, Christmas 1923*, is written by a "Dunhillite," in a literary style reminiscent of J.M. Barrie's *My Lady Nicotine*. A most unique and so Dunhill-like eccentric yet classy production. The second book—a little jewel nestled in a back-cover pocket—is Dunhill's WWI 1914 Christmas catalogue for the soldier and sailor campaigning abroad, *Things The Soldiers are Asking For!* Dunhill ephemera at its best! Available as a special, limited release Christmastime 2010. $25

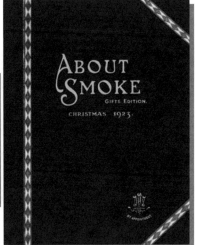

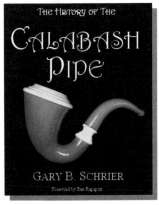

The History of the Calabash Pipe by Gary B. Schrier

The author's magnum opus. The only authoritative guide for the pipeman with a penchant for that eccentric, quintessentially English-looking pipe, the calabash. A never-before-told story of the most fascinating pipe ever conceived. Critically acclaimed by knowledgeable pipemen the world over. A must have. Completely revised and updated second printing. With a foreword by Ben Rapaport. Available Christmastime 2011.

www.briarbooks.com

Briar Books Press
Fine books for the pipeman

Introduces...

THE PIPEMAN'S LIBRARY

Nothing goes better with a "pipe" than a book (save perhaps a good single malt Scotch!). And what better to read while smoking than about pipes and tobacco, the lifestyle, the characters, and the history. Buy books from Briar Books Press from the comfort and camaraderie of your **PIPE CLUB** ... and save money.

It is my belief that for a pipe club to be of benefit to its members it must offer safe haven; it must entertain; it must be sufficiently financed; and it must elevate the interests and aspirations of all to a higher order of knowledge of the pipe and tobacco, their use, history, and absolute enjoyment. I created THE PIPEMAN'S LIBRARY to meet these needs. Ten years ago, I also co-created a thriving pipe club in Seattle, where many of its members have purchased my books. I think the Seattle boys are the most erudite pipemen in the country! Join in their experience: buy quality pipe books to build your own Pipeman's Library. And why not make an event of it at your next meeting. —GARY B. SCHRIER, PUBLISHER

Here's How it Works

Your club will be sent a full set of Briar Books Press titles for your meeting. Books are reviewed; orders are taken. The order and funds are remitted. Your club receives its order in time for the next meeting along with a check made out to the club for 15% of the value of the order. Briar Books Press pays the shipping! It's brilliant! Visit the web site to get the full details.

www.briarbooks.com